Queerly Connected

Queerly Connected

*A Spouse's First-Year Journey
Navigating Love & Identity in Transition*

Nuranissa M. Jones

Queerly Connected copyright © 2024 by Nuranissa M. Jones, all rights reserved.

Formatting by Bent Elbow Press

This book is a compilation of the author's life and experiences. Any resemblance to another person's life, business establishments, locales, or persons, living or dead, is entirely coincidental.

All rights reserved. No part of this publication may be reproduced, stored in a retrieval system, or transmitted in any form or by any means (electronic, mechanical, photocopying, recording, or otherwise) without the priority written permission of both the copyright owner and the publisher. The only exception is brief quotations in printed reviews.

The scanning, uploading, and distribution of this book via the internet or via any other means without the permission of the publisher and author is illegal and punishable by law. Please purchase only authorized electronic editions or paper copies, and do not participate in or encourage electronic piracy of copyrighted materials. Your support of the author's rights is appreciated.

Book Description

Nuranissa M. Jones thought she had everything figured out—married to the love of her life and mother to three children. Her world seemed complete. Unexpectedly, her spouse made a heartfelt discovery about their true gender identity and shared it with her. *Queerly Connected: A Spouse's First Year Journey Navigating Love and Identity in Transition* shares Jones's journey from identifying as a lesbian to embracing a queer identity, as her spouse transitioned from female to male (ftm). This story is Jones's lived experience—an exploration filled with humor and the heart of what it means to love and live authentically while supporting her trans spouse. This book will connect deeply with anyone who has loved ones facing gender transition, offering hope, insight, and the affirmation that love can adapt and thrive in the face of profound change.

This book is dedicated to all individuals and couples navigating the profound journey of a spouse's transition. May you find strength and love in your paths, just as we have found in ours.

Acknowledgments

This book is a reflection of the journeys we went through together, not alone. I am immensely grateful to my editor, who helped me every step of the way in shaping the narrative you read today. She pushed me to dig deeper into my authentic experiences, helping me to clearly express what I was truly thinking and feeling. Her guidance was essential in organizing my initial scattered 50 pages into a coherent story, one that others could understand and connect with. She helped me get clear with my core message and focus on the story I wanted to tell and the major challenges within it.

Equally, I greatly appreciate my spouse's support. His encouragement to continue writing, even when revisiting painful memories, and his acceptance of sharing our story is inspiring. He is not only an incredible partner and parent but also an inspiration who continually supports my dreams as we strive to support each other's aspirations. I am unbelievably lucky to share this life and its dreams with him.

My heartfelt thanks also go to my closest friends. From day one, they have been **incredible** sources of support, being there for me through thick and thin, and celebrating every step of the way with me. I wish I could name you by name, but I hope you know who you are!

I am beyond grateful to my **amazing** friends in my book club. You have been **so supportive**, and I am so grateful to have you in my life. Your friendship and insightful feedback have been crucial in refining this manuscript. You've reminded me that this is a story that needs to be told and helped me silence the negative chatter in my head, encouraging me to just keep going.

I must also express my profound gratitude to Apa, whose unconditional love and encouragement have supported me throughout this journey. We would not be the family we are without you.

Finally, I want to thank the greater community of friends and families that have accepted and shown us unconditional love. Thank you all for being part of this journey.

Contents

CHAPTER 1	1
CHAPTER 2	7
December	
CHAPTER 3	23
January	
CHAPTER 4	31
Part I	
February 2001	31
PART II	39
February Present Day	39
CHAPTER 5	69
March	
CHAPTER 6	93
April	
CHAPTER 7	111
May	
CHAPTER 8	123
June	
CHAPTER 9	127
July	
CHAPTER 10	131
August	
CHAPTER 11	139
September	
CHAPTER 12	149
October	
CHAPTER 13	173
November	

CHAPTER 14 191
December and Beyond

APPENDIX

Shifts in Intimacy 209
Organizing Friend and Reader Groups 215
First Book Club Agenda One 223
Second Book Club Agenda Two 225
Helpful Literature Resources by Topic 229

About the Author 233

Chapter 1

I came out as a lesbian to my mother while she was chopping onions before school one day. I was fifteen. She responded with momentary sadness, saying I wouldn't raise children. (Ha! Three kids later!) She then offered to drive me to school. She told me she loved me no matter what. Little did I know at 40, after building a life I could love, my world and identity would be shaken, and I wouldn't know who I was anymore. Of course, my surprise was nothing compared to my spouse's shock when he realized he was trans and not a lesbian at all.

When Jay began questioning his gender, I was a whirlwind of emotions. I had so many questions. None of them had simple answers. Am *I* a lesbian still? Can our relationship survive this? Could I be as happy with a man as I had been with a woman? If I'm married to a man, what is my identity?

What about the kids? Will *they* be okay? What will they

think about all of this? And our extended families? Will they be supportive?

What I knew was I wanted us to stay together. I didn't have a question about my love for my spouse. I did, though, have a million worries about how to make this work as a couple. I had identified as a lesbian for over 25 years. As Jay was discovering and becoming himself, all I could do was respond with an overwhelming storm of emotions that included everything from elation for him to fear and anxiety to my own deep sorrow. I wanted to support Jay in becoming himself, but I didn't know what that meant for me. Or our family. Or our relationship.

I had built my life around certain ideas about myself and our relationship that I learned during Jay's coming out were not grounded in reality. I realized I had built a foundation of emotional stability on Jay being my wife. Growing up, my mother struggled with major depressive episodes, and my father struggled with volatile emotions. I responded by making sure everything in my life was as stable as possible. Jay's transition threatened that stability.

A gender realization affects the dreams, understandings and memories of the past, present and future in profound ways. A transition doesn't just change the future of a relationship. It significantly alters the way we view the past as well.

It is like finding out you have been wearing blue-tinted glasses during your entire relationship and they explained how everything in your life was perceived. Taking off the glasses and putting on a clear pair can at first feel like looking at yourself in a funhouse mirror. Then, over time, one realizes how much better the clear glasses are. What you see is now much closer to reality. You might see problems that were hidden before. With clear vision, the new challenges can be addressed and solved. Or the new problems can be addressed and kept in the realm of unsolvable but acceptable. But either way, it's better than looking through the world through colored glasses that hide reality.

While this book is about my part in the discovery process, Jay's own journey was also unique and challenging beyond belief. To this day, I am in awe of Jay's vulnerability, strength and commitment to fully be himself. I love Jay more than it's possible to imagine. This process, in the end, helped us both live more authentically. Now, I can't imagine our life any other way. But there were many hard moments to figure out. Moments where I felt alive, anxious, depressed, and totally lost. This book is about how I made it through all these stages and found more stability than I ever had before.

As I set out to share some of what I learned, I hope to ease some of your fears of transition as a spouse or partner. Even if you do not have a trans spouse yourself, you probably have had moments in your life where everything changed unexpectedly. Change doesn't affect only you, but the whole family. And at the end of the day, it affects the marriage and non-transitioning partner on a level that is inconceivable to many people who have not experienced it.

Some questions I hope to answer in this book are:
What was it like? What were the hard parts? What was

helpful? What wasn't helpful? What can you do when you feel like the emotions are too much to bear? How do you keep calm for the children and be supportive for the family? How do you embrace all the emotions—both the grief and feelings of loss, along with the joy of discovery?

Jay transitioning has turned out to be one of the best things that has happened to us. He is happier and more himself. I sometimes find it hard to believe that there was a time before we knew he was Jay. That time feels further and further away and more and more surreal with each passing day. Every so often I catch a glance at a picture of who he used to be, and I wonder how did he live like that? How could neither of us see that something was up?

My message of our story is only from one side. I can't share Jay's perspective—which is, of course, very different from mine. But I will share what helped me and how we navigated this huge transition as a family. I will focus on my experience during the first year of Jay's transition—when I had the most adjusting to do. That first year was challenging, exciting, and unlike any other year in my life, and I hope as you read about my journey, you will find a sense of connection between our experiences that will help you find the joy in your journey too.

I've organized this book by time—from month one to twelve, so you can get a sense of the pace on how things changed in our lives. If you have a partner, family member, or friend transitioning, they might move in a faster, slower, or totally different direction. I hope my perspective is helpful.

After month twelve, I share an epilogue that includes a

few thoughts from between years one and five. In this section, I also share my top tips for coping and thriving through change.

The last chapter is a how-to chapter on creating new friendships with people who have a shared experience. It is the rare and special friend who really understands how beautiful, awesome, unsettling and world-rocking a transition can be for the person who is not transitioning in a relationship. I made many friends to help me along the way, and that made all the difference. I wish to share how I did that so you, too, can form new friendships to help you along this journey.

I hope in this story you see some of your experiences reflected. And if you don't see them, I hope you share your own story in whatever way works for you.

In the beginning, though, I didn't have anyone to talk to. I had read no stories that reflected what I was going through. I felt very alone and confused. Later, I wrote this book for others to know they aren't alone. This is the book and connection I wish I had.

Chapter 2

December

One cloudy Pacific Northwest afternoon in early December, my spouse Jay and my youngest daughter Joan were joyfully splashing outside in our hot tub. The jacuzzi was new—a present for my 40th birthday, which had happened earlier that year. Jay and I splurged on this gift that was both practical and sentimental. Practical because I love soaking in hot water. But also, the hot tub connected to an emotional memory from our very first date. But more on that later.

Our youngest child and Jay were in the hot tub, and he eventually came in to get ready for dinner while Joan kept on swimming. I was in the kitchen preparing the dinner for the night. As Jay toweled off, he started chatting with me. Liz, our middle daughter, was in the family room, next to the kitchen, coloring on an iPad app.

"I had a thought while I was in the hot tub," Jay said.

"Really? What about?" I asked while standing in the kitchen pouring myself a glass of water.

I was expecting him to say something like, "Why don't we get new carpets? The ones we have are looking really old." Or maybe he would say, "You know how I want us to visit a bunch of national and state parks before the kids go off to college? That time is coming up faster than we realized. Let's visit Crater Lake this fall." I was expecting some sort of normal, everyday conversation topic.

Not something that would change our lives forever.

"I was thinking about all the trans people I follow on Instagram."

"Yeah?" I responded, wondering where this was going. He followed many trans people on Instagram. Every so often he would tell me about the people he was following: a schoolteacher from a southern state that transitioned from male to female and her challenges and triumphs at school, a family with five children in Canada where one parent transitioned from female to male. The stories were interesting and inspiring to hear about.

"Well. What if I'm not just an ally?" Jay asked.

"Not just an ally?" I repeated, not completely understanding.

"What if I have more in common than I realized with the trans people I follow?"

What??? I thought.

This is not the type of thought *I* would just state out of the blue. If I had a thought like this, I would mull it over for days or weeks before saying anything out loud. But Jay isn't like that. It's part of what I love about him. He just says what he's thinking.

Liz apparently had been listening to this whole conversation because she piped up from the living room at this moment. I almost hadn't remembered she was nearby in the living room. She was sitting down on the couch doing a coloring app on an iPad. She was so quiet; it was like she wasn't in the room. But clearly Liz had been paying attention to the entire conversation.

"You are a lady, Mama. You are a lady," she said to Jay forcefully.

I said, "Let's talk about this more later, after the kids go to bed, ok?"

Somehow, I put the conversation out of my mind for the rest of the evening. I'm not sure how that was possible in retrospect. Actually, it wasn't until writing this book that Jay reminded me of this first conversation. He clearly remembered it. I only remembered the discussion from after dinner.

After dinner, and the bedtime marathon, it was time to chat more about Jay's epiphany. What I am sharing is my best memory of what happened. Mostly, I was curious about what was going on. Part of me was terrified of what I was about to hear, but I knew no matter what, I wanted the details.

As Jay talked, I could hear my heart beating during his every word. But then I felt a deep calmness spread throughout my body. This moment was not about me. This was big, whatever was going on. I've had previous times in my life where I had to deal with an unexpected situation, like a student getting their finger stuck in a swinging metal grate on the playground. I tend to remain calm when something unexpected happens. Time slows down, and I stay focused on the moment. All the normal chatter in my head quiets down and I'm just present. This was one of those times for me.

"It was just that…I don't know what it means. It doesn't have to mean anything," Jay tried to explain. "I mean, nothing has to change. It's not like I'm trans or anything like that. I mean. I don't know. I just know I don't feel like a female. I don't know what I feel like."

I listened quietly. In my mind, all was still at this moment. I held him and did my best to listen to my spouse.

I'm sure my silence had Jay worried and thinking what were my thoughts? Was I freaking out inside?

Jay turned the conversation fast, saying, "I don't have to make any changes."

I believe he was so concerned about hurting me and our family that he denied what he was really feeling. I probably would have had the same concerns if the situation were reversed. I might have offered the same response.

Generally, big changes have not been positive for me, and Jay knew this. For years, Jay had been trying to convince me we should paint one of our rooms a different color. Maybe just the ceiling. I had a hard time envisioning how the different color would look, and I loved the deep red color we had, even if it was a bit too dark. After many years, I agreed for us to paint just part of the ceiling a lighter color, so half of our dining room wasn't so dark. The rest of the walls are still red in the room, just half the ceiling was changed. Turns out, the new ceiling was so much better. But it took a lot of resistance from me to get there.

Jay, having the epiphany that he was more than an ally with his social media follows, was a little bigger than changing the ceiling color of our dining room. I don't remember what we did after we talked, but sometime later that night, we got ready for bed. Jay and I cuddled for a while, but I felt restless. I like to journal when my thoughts are busy, and so I got up and wrote a bit. Normally when writing I'll free associate and write three pages or more at a time. This night, I only wrote two sentences.

What if Sophia is really a man and not a lesbian? That honestly sounds scary.

(I didn't use the name he would eventually take, obviously, nor his actual birth name. At that moment, neither of us knew he would change his name. To keep this story as true to my experience as possible, I am using a female name as I did in my writings that night, but I'm using a pseudonym.)

When I reread the sentences while writing this book, I was shocked. In my mind, I had "remembered" I wrote what if *I'm* not a lesbian? But it turns out on that fateful day, my biggest fear was that Jay wasn't a lesbian. Because in my mind, that would mean he would leave me.

My fear of him leaving me would be one of the more painful aspects of this early part of the transition for Jay. I wish I could go back and spare both of us the experience of those fears, but I can't.

After the not-quite-coming-out conversation, I only had a few more days of work before my holiday vacation began. My teaching schedule was perfect that year. I had one week where I was off from school, but our children were still in school. This gave me an extra week for myself.

That week together was really special. Those days before the winter holidays (we celebrate Hanukkah and Christmas) Jay and I talked and connected, as we prepared for the holidays. One day that week, we went on a hike in the woods. There is a nature area close to our house. We drove over to the nature paths and walked on a bike/walk trail along a creek with our dog Tango. As we were walking, I asked how Jay was feeling. Did he feel non-binary, or was he a trans guy? Or something else?

"So, do you feel like a guy?" I questioned.

He still wasn't sure.

"How long have you felt this way?"

Walking with our dog, holding hands, he tried his best to put what he was experiencing into words. It was a sudden realization while, at the same time, had always been there under the surface, only noticeable in retrospect.

Looking back through our relationship, this made sense. When Jay and I met, he presented androgynously. On occasions, he would even be mistaken for a guy, which he really did not like. Over time, though, he stopped dressing quite so androgynously and started to wear more mom clothes as we had children.

Walking along, hand in hand, he answered my questions the best that he could. But there were many things he just didn't know yet about himself.

At the time I kept wondering if Jay coming out as trans meant that he would no longer be attracted to me. No matter how many times Jay reassured me (and he did over and over) that his attraction for me had nothing to do with his gender identity, I just couldn't really grasp what he was saying.

On top of that, I was confused about what this realization meant for my own identity. Would I still be a lesbian? Also, if he wasn't a woman, would I continue to be attracted to him both physically and emotionally? I couldn't comprehend how this all would work out. But I tried to understand and be loving in the best way I could through my confusion.

Walking in the nature park, that day, a few things were clear to me. I still loved my spouse dearly. And... he needed a new wardrobe. Non-binary or trans, the clothes he was wearing were not pleasing to his newfound sense of self.

So, after the walk, I suggested we go to Target to pick up some Christmas presents for him on our way home. Normally, clothes shopping was something we both avoided. Me, because I just really hate clothes shopping—the overhead fluorescent lighting, the noise, and it simply boggles my mind that some people shop because it is fun, and Jay, because he was shopping in the wrong department! Jay typically found the most acceptable of what he didn't like and was out of the women's department in a flash.

At the store, we strolled past the dollar deals, the women's clothes section, past the bras and women's active wear to the very back of the store, to the men's section.

Jay's face lit up. There were so many choices: jeans that did not accentuate hips, athletic shorts, sweatpants in dark colors, button-downs with different color plaid, and more. For one of the first times ever, he looked happy shopping for himself.

We didn't know what size would fit Jay. We went into the boys' department, and he tried a range of sizes. We found a variety of pants, none of which hugged his body. In the end, we found new jeans and athletic pants for Jay... all with real pockets. (Ok, why in the world don't women's clothes have decent pockets? Just saying, totally not fair.) We found some button-down shirts and some other shirts as well. I had never seen Jay excited about shopping before, except when he helped pick out clothes for me or for our three children.

Jay looked radiant in his new finds. I couldn't bear to make him wait all the way to Christmas to have all the new outfits. Some purchases we kept out so Jay could start wearing clothes that made him feel good on the inside right away. Other items we stored away so they could be his Christmas presents that year.

That special week went by, and then our extended families arrived for the holidays. It was time for us to make gingerbread houses, light the Menorah, and celebrate. This year our gingerbread house featured a hot tub out back and a red licorice pathway.

The Christmas tree was decorated with many unique ornaments, including the ornament Jay and I bought from a New Age store on our very first date night after our oldest child was born—an iridescent butterfly.

For one of our holiday get-togethers, I put on a dress. I can still remember standing in our closet looking at myself in the full-length mirror. This dress twirled if I spun around in circles. I took a spin just for some fun and smiled at Jay, who was buttoning up his shirt.

Spinning around, feeling the fluttering fabric, I had a question for Jay. "You really never enjoyed wearing a dress? Not even just to turn and make it twirl?"

"Um. No." Jay looked at me like I had just grown a horn on my head.

Wow, I thought. It never occurred to me he would feel differently about something that was so clear to me.

But now, seeing Jay looking at himself in the mirror wearing his new clothes, something dawned on me. I had never seen Jay admire himself in the mirror before. He really looked great and was so much more comfortable in his new clothes. He looked more like how he used to dress when we met, before we had kids. There was a familiarity and newness to everything at the same time.

Christmas arrived, and the kids bounded down the stairs, excited to open their stockings. Santa filled them with lots of cute toys—bubbles, silly putty, fun socks and other little presents to enjoy before breakfast. After eating the Christmas Casserole and fresh pears, it was finally time for the presents. Both sets of grandparents sat down on the couches and the kids and I sat on the ground. Gifts were passed out and paper ripped and presents opened. Jay received the clothes from me he chose earlier that month.

Having everyone around felt both wonderful and overwhelming. Obviously, no one in the extended family knew what was up. It was stressful having everyone there and trying to keep this a secret. I felt like I needed to act like everything was normal and I was totally fine. The kids had no clue. Somehow, Liz seemed to have forgotten the conversation and her insistence that "Mama was a lady." Amazingly, no one appeared to think anything about all the clothing I gave Jay for Christmas. He liked androgynous clothes, and people were focused on their own presents.

The secret was a lot to hold on to. Acting as if everything was normal, not really knowing how Jay was going to identify. I felt like a bundle of confusion. I just wanted some clarity, but I was afraid of what that clarity would bring. What would things be like next Christmas? Who would Jay be next Christmas?

I needed some way to express myself. I did some writing, but mostly that seemed to bring up all the uncertainty. For once, writing wasn't soothing.

I also turned to meditation. Normally, following my breath helps me while I'm feeling overwhelmed. But calming my mind wasn't working very well. It was just too busy with thoughts and worries about the future. I needed something to calm me down.

What I found was music.

Chapter 2

I turned to learning new songs to play on the piano. When I learn new pieces, my mind is fully focused on the task at hand and nothing else. While sitting at the keys, I have my back to the rest of the family, which offers some space. Jay bought the piano for me 18 years earlier, the first significant gift he ever gave me. The instrument has been in two apartments and three houses with me. So, during the winter break, when the socializing and acting like everything was normal became too much, I sat at the piano and practiced new songs. Through music, I channeled all my confusion and excitement and fear. I played, expressing all my loneliness, fear, and wonder at what would come through the songs.

When Christmas was over, the festivities continued. My birthday happened in the next few days, along with Jay and my meetiversary. For my birthday, we decided to go bowling as a family.

As we found our lane and got settled, I looked around and noticed a family bowling next to us with kids. The guy next to us looked like he was around Jay's build. The guy had a beard and was there with his wife and kids. He had similar hair coloring to Jay. Every so often, between strikes and pizza, I glanced over at the couple next to me. I tried to imagine, could I find Jay attractive if he looked like that? Could I find the guy attractive if I tried? Maybe? Not really.

My attraction to Jay was an instantaneous experience. I didn't need to think about it. I can remember him walking up to the doors of my house in Oakland so many years ago and being awestruck by him immediately. I can still see him strolling up the sidewalk to the stairs for the first time. I see his shaven head, piercing eyes, and warm smile. It ignited a tingling, an alive feeling.

I couldn't manufacture that for the guy at the bowling alley. Or honestly, for most any other guy I attempted to look at in that way. I could imagine attraction, but not the gut feelings.

I had my serious doubts about what would happen if Jay changed to look like the man he felt on the inside. Jay looked way more androgynous when we met, and I was totally attracted to that. Until this point, my attraction toward him had never been a significant issue, no matter how he looked. He has gained weight, lost weight, gotten pregnant, and built his muscles and through it all, I have continued to find him attractive. I preferred some looks over others, but I loved him no matter what.

I had my worries about what would happen to my attraction if he eventually decided he wanted to take testosterone when he realized he was a guy. But as best I could, I focused on the bowling and the here and now. After some rounds, we headed home and celebrated with a homemade chocolate cake, made by Jay, who had wanted to be a pastry chef when he was a kid.

A few days after the winter holiday celebrations, the extended family departed. It was quieter and calmer in the house. I needed that space to decompress. I felt numb and overwhelmed and happy and sad and everything all at once. I kept on practicing the piano daily, sometimes multiple times a day. But I needed more than just music to get through this. I needed some support.

Chapter 2

There was no one outside of Jay I felt I could talk to. It wasn't fair for me to go to Jay for comfort, since he was the one going through this realization. But I couldn't talk with any of our friends without outing Jay. I needed to find a therapist.

One evening, I went online to Psychology Today to look for a therapist. I typed in certain criteria to find someone who might be able to help. I found a person who said they ran a support group for people that had trans and non-binary spouses. That sounded amazing.

This therapist was the only option that I could find in my city, so hopefully she was good! There were lots of therapists that worked with people who were transitioning, but no one else appeared to focus on spouses. The website said she had a support group for people who wanted to stay married and that she followed a counseling method called The Gottman Method.

I had heard of The Gottman Method before. I knew it was a researched-based approach to relationship counseling. Knowing about this method seemed like a sign that she was the person for me.

When I was in high school, my parents attended a training with the Gottmans and brought home the book, *Why Marriages Succeed or Fail*. Even though I was only about 17 at the time, I read parts of the book one day. It was eye-opening. Unlike a lot of other relationship books, it broke down communication to the sentence level. It talked a lot about this idea of bids for attention and that in any healthy relationship (including friendship) people respond to the other person's bid for connection. One example the book gave for relationships that stayed together was: if your spouse says, "Look at the bird outside," the other person would respond to the comment most of the time. In the relationships that would end in divorce, often the comment would be ignored. It was unlike any other book I had read before. I often had a hard time making and keeping friends in high school, college and beyond. Finally, someone was laying out some real specific ideas for how to build friendships. I would go on to read quite a few other books written by the Gottmans.

Now, if this therapist was trained by the Gottmans, I thought that hopefully I would be in good hands. This spouse's support group seemed like a good possibility. I filled out the online form to request more information. And waited.

A few days before New Year's Eve, Jay and I had a date night. A babysitter watched the kids while Jay and I went to a Korean BBQ with a good friend of ours. Earlier that same day, Jay went to get drinks with the husband of a former classmate who had transitioned.

While Jay was away having drinks, my mind filled with nervous chatter. What were they talking about? I was going to meet Jay after he talked with this person. I left the kids with our babysitter and drove to the Korean BBQ restaurant. It was a rainy, somewhat gloomy evening. I waited in the parking lot for Jay to arrive, but he and our friend arrived around the same time. We didn't have any time to talk before dinner.

During dinner, I tried to stay focused on our friend and chatting about our winter breaks, kids and our summer plans, but underneath, I really wanted our friend to go so I could hear about how the meet-up had gone.

After dinner, Jay and I went to sit in his car for a few minutes of privacy. Even though we drove in separate cars, we sat in the minivan together under some streetlights. In the parking lot outside of a suburban mall, Jay came out again with more clarity. He told me he realized he was a trans guy, and not non-binary. As he was talking with his former classmate's husband (who would become one of his good friends) the pieces just clicked.

Maybe it helped that his friend, like us, had children and was married to his wife prior to transitioning. Maybe it helped that they were both over 40. Maybe the time was just right for Jay to acknowledge something that I had already suspected.

I was surprised, and yet I was not surprised all.

I didn't expect the initial conversations about gender prior to his hot tub realization. But at the same time, ever since he said he was questioning his gender, I was convinced he would end up realizing he was a guy. I had seen that it was coming, at least for a short time.

I was excited, but I was terrified. I loved Jay as he was. I was afraid of how things would change, and yet I wanted Jay to be happy.

So, eighteen years plus two days after we met, I found out that the person I met was actually a guy. Surprise!

Like a Christmas miracle (though it was almost New Year's), the therapist who ran the support group for spouses of trans individuals called me that very evening.

Jay had already gone to bed, and I was sitting up in

front of our gas insert fireplace. I had so many thoughts in my head that I couldn't really fall asleep. An unknown number called and while I normally wouldn't have answered the phone, I did that evening. It was the therapist!

She asked me how I was doing and what had been going on. It was nice to have someone other than Jay to talk to. I had so many thoughts in my mind and had been holding quite a few of them in. She listened and reassured me that many other people had been through this and felt the same way I did. Most couples who wanted to stay together could. After listening and answering a few of my questions, she did a screening call with me to see if I qualified to join the trans spouse support group.

During the screening call, I expressed my concern over my identity. Was I still a lesbian? How would I now identify? Other than a few failed attempts to date guys, I realized at an early age that I wasn't into them. So, who would I be if my spouse transitioned to one? Would I stay attracted to him?

I strongly remember the therapist saying that everyone worries about that in the beginning. Everyone is concerned about how they now label themselves, and that is normal. She said I might not believe it now, but in time, these issues would no longer be such a big worry for me. I would just be concerned with living and being with my spouse, and the label I used would matter a lot less. Other things would become much more important.

I didn't really believe her, but I hoped she was correct. I would soon find out.

Chapter 3

January

The time between when I talked with the therapist and attended my first trans spouse support group felt like it stretched on forever. In the meantime, Jay and I went to a local bookstore as part of a date night. We both looked for some books about other people who had transitioned. I didn't feel like I could talk with anyone, but maybe I could find a connection in a book.

I remember feeling self-conscious, excited, and concerned while walking down the aisle. I wanted assurance that everything would be ok. I wanted to understand what was going on with Jay and what he was feeling. I hoped to find a book that would help me understand and guide me through this process. The internet didn't have too many uplifting stories. A few of the stories online shared how when some transitioned from female to male (ftm) sometimes the individual shifted their own sexuality as they took hormones. This was not calming to me at all.

I hoped I could find a story of another spouse in a similar situation and how they had managed this transition or a book from the perspective of someone like Jay so I could understand better.

There were not a lot of books to choose from, and some books we found actually made me more anxious. I worried more and more that I would lose the person I loved if he transitioned, that he would turn into someone quite different. Some books talked about how people had less access to emotions as they started T, and that terrified me. I hoped the therapy group would offer some reassurance about our relationship that I wasn't receiving from those books.

During the time leading up to the group, I was working and trying to live my life as normally as possible. I attempted to be there for the kids, hold everything together and act like nothing was going on. All of that took an emotional toll on me. I couldn't hold it in all the time and needed a release valve.

One day, driving to work, I was suddenly overcome with grief and started sobbing. I cried so hard I couldn't see and had to pull over to the side of the road. The sobs coming out of me were unlike any sound I had ever heard before. Was this really happening to me? This was a strange dream, right?

A few minutes later, I pulled myself back together and drove the rest of the way to work, trying to put those feelings aside. Being at my job was a great distraction. I worked as a Spanish teacher at a local public school. The nice thing about teaching 30 children in a room, talking in

Chapter 3

a second language and managing behavior, curriculum, and everything else is there is no time for personal thoughts. So, once I got to work, within ten minutes, I could just focus on my job. This gave me a needed break from my emotional roller coaster of concerns.

The week dragged on, but I made it through. Finally, Sunday arrived—the day for my very first trans spouse support group! I woke up a bundle of nerves, skipped breakfast and kissed Jay goodbye. Jay also felt anxious about the group, wondering if it would be helpful for me and make things easier. Or would I learn something that would make things harder for us?

I left the house early, parking outside of the church, now turned into a community center where the group was held and met the therapist at the door. We walked through a poorly lit old-fashioned chapel to narrow wooden stairs to the infant nursery on the top floor. The label on the door read *Cry Room*.

I walked inside with the therapist and met a few other spouses. There were about five or six people all together. The room was a bit cold, but there were lots of pillows and blankets and tea. I made myself a cup and sat down.

Everyone introduced themselves and shared a little about their situations. I think I went last. But when I tried to talk, I couldn't. I just cried. It was so hard for me to get through. I couldn't voice what was happening in my situation without sobbing.

And so, in that first session, I listened.

Everyone seemed so nice and so much more together than me. Some people had known for close to a decade, others for just a few months or years. Even the newer people seemed light-years ahead of me.

My first question I asked was about hormones and if they changed their partner's sexual orientation. After reading on the internet that some people shift with hormones, this was my biggest fear. I couldn't get the idea out of my head. Would Jay become a gay man? Would he no longer be attracted to me? I was attracted to him, but what if that changed for him?

The group was unanimous.

When you have a strong relationship and are committed to staying together, the transitioning spouse almost always continues to be attracted to the non-transitioning spouse. Generally, most problems could be overcome with support and therapy. The therapist had worked with lots of couples, and this wasn't a huge concern.

They all agreed that occasionally the transition spouse shifted their own sexual orientation. But if Jay said he was still attracted to me, I really didn't need to worry about that. What a relief. Even though Jay had been saying this, I needed to hear it from other spouses who were further along than me.

At the end of the first meeting, the therapist offered to teach a technique to handle strong emotions. The technique was called tapping. It involved tapping different body parts like the temples and head while speaking affirmations like "Even though I don't think I can, I CAN handle this".

While tapping the specific spots, I let myself let go of my overwhelming thoughts and feelings. Now I had a plan for what to do when grief overpowered me, like what had happened the first week while I was driving to work. I could choose to stay with the feelings. Sobbing and crying. Crying and sobbing. Releasing. Over five or ten minutes of tapping, I would start to feel better.

I released emotions I had been avoiding, my fear and sadness. I felt a greater sense of trust in our relationship. This was possible. We could get through this. It might be tough, but there was hope for us.

Leaving the support group, I felt so much more optimistic about everything. I knew I loved Jay, and he loved me. Other people had been down this journey and were happier now than they had been before.

I arrived at home to find Jay waiting nervously about what I was going to say. He was relieved that I found the group helpful and that I had found some support. I explained to him about tapping and that it was normal for spouses to feel a wide range of emotions, including grief. I think it helped him to know that me experiencing sadness was a part of the healing process and was totally normal. All the other spouses went through this phase, too. But it wouldn't last forever.

The following weeks, I had some moments of deep grief. I would be fine and suddenly a thought storm would hit me like a wave. "Jay is going to want to take testosterone and then he is going to be closed off to his feelings and then he will be like someone else and I will lose the person I love." I would get caught in this obsessive loop, thinking the same things over and over, feeling more and more upset. When they crashed on me, I would go up into my closet and take ten minutes to tap. I felt guilty that I was feeling sad. But my therapist kept telling me that avoiding my emotions would make things worse. I need to let the feelings crash over me and float on them. No matter how silly I felt.

My routine looked like the following. I would let Jay know I needed a few minutes in the closet. I would close the door behind me and sit on the floor facing a full-length mirror and tap. Pretty soon I moved from saying the set phrases my therapist gave me to just saying thoughts that popped into my mind. I let go and didn't censor myself. It wasn't necessarily the way the therapist taught me to do the technique, but it worked for me.

I spent a lot of time in the closet that January! Me, going back into the closet to deal with my spouse coming out of the closet. It felt so silly. Every so often, I would laugh at the irony of the situation. Life definitely has a sense of humor.

But, week after week, I realized I cried less. Though it wasn't like a linear line—more like a wave that trended downward over time. I learned to process those sad feelings away from Jay as much as possible.

Some time that month, Jay suggested I should reach out to one of my close friends to talk about everything. He agreed to let me share about what was happening with one of my best friends, Sarah. I was hesitant to talk with any friends because almost all my friends also know Jay. I didn't want him to be outed before he was ready. But I needed someone to talk with at the same time, someone who really knew me. The therapy group was helpful, but

Chapter 3

none of those people knew our relationship or me from before.

Sarah and I planned to meet up at her house after school. After work, I remember driving to my friend's house. I had "'Tis a Gift to be Simple" by Yo Yo Ma playing on repeat in the car. Tears flowed down my face through the music. I was happy to be talking with Sarah, as it made everything feel more real to share about it. But I also felt overwhelmed by all my feelings. Sarah and I met over a decade prior, and we were couple-friends with Sarah and her wife.

That afternoon, I believe I talked with Sarah for over two hours. I cried. I shared my fears. I talked and talked, and my best friend witnessed my pain, my fears, my hopes and me. She let me be vulnerable and be myself.

Having a friend to talk with brought me significant comfort. Being able to talk with someone who really knew me and my family and Jay prior to transition helped me in more ways than I can express in words. I felt seen. I did not feel so alone.

Later, after talking with Sarah and attending my therapy group, Jay found a book that better described his experience. He discovered the book *The Tomboy Survival Guide* by Ivan Coyote. Jay devoured the book and underlined and highlighted parts where he resonated with Ivan's experience. Then he gave me the book to read, noticing where he underlined was like a breath of fresh air to me.

Many things that the author described made sense to me at a deep level. In reading Ivan's story, Jay's experiences made more sense to me. This was a story I could relate to. It gave me a vision of who Jay could be. This book, along with my support group and a friend to be real with, provided me a glimpse of a future I could be excited about.

I felt hopeful for that future to come.

Chapter 4

Part I

February 2001

Before I go into the vision of how our life would progress post-transition, I want to take you back to our first February 14th together.

We had only been dating around 8 weeks and were living in California at the time when we celebrated our first Valentine's Day in 2001. I surprised Jay by blindfolding him and taking him to a restaurant called Autumn Moon Cafe in Oakland, CA. We ate outside in a garden, savoring French toast, mochas, and the butterflies of a new fluttering relationship.

After we ate and were back at the car, Jay surprised me by putting the blindfold on me! He drove for what seemed like forever. I could feel the car moving up and down hills, around turns. I eventually asked if we were at the Oakland Zoo, after so many twists and turns, but he stopped at some place I had never been—Tilden Park, a pretty park in the East Bay of San Francisco Bay Area. He took me to ride on a steam train, an activity he did as a child with his grandmother.

Jay and I met on Craigslist just eight weeks before that first Valentine's Day. Earlier in December, I posted a Craigslist ad saying I was not looking for love, but just cuddles.

I lived in a shared roommate situation, but it wasn't right for me. The house had shared cooking duties, a hot tub, and was near my school where I taught sixth grade math, science and reading. I loved the way the house looked and liked everyone in the house. Unfortunately, my roommates were all a good decade older and more mature than me!

Barely surviving my first years of teaching, I had little time to give to the co-op. Most of the fall, I had been struggling with depression and anxiety, and barely made it through each day. I didn't have much energy left over to socialize and be an extroverted, upbeat housemate. What I needed after a day of work was a place where I could relax, be myself and not be social. But I can see in retrospect that a lot of the reasons the house wasn't a good fit had to do with how stressed I was at work.

As a housemate, I could be a bit flaky–though probably no more than the average 20-year-old. I forgot to pick up the Community Supported Agriculture box one too many times. I didn't help in the "optional" work parties, which I thought actually were optional. They weren't! I didn't

Chapter 4

socialize enough with everyone else. I just didn't "fit into the co-op culture."

So, after some discussions with my roommates, I decided to search for a new living situation, looking on Craigslist for a new room to rent.

Around the same time, I explored polyamory and all things queer in the Bay Area. I was dating a woman who lived near me who was also dating many other people at the same time. I tried going on a bunch of dates from different online sites. Sometimes I danced with a lesbian country and western dance group.

Dating seemed hopeless.

I would never meet the love of my life, I thought. That just happens in fairy tales. So at 22, I sort of gave up on the idea of finding love. I figured, well, maybe the whole love thing is outside my control. But what did I want? I wanted someone to be affectionate with and to cuddle with. I thought I didn't really need sex, just a nice person to cuddle with.

While looking on Craigslist for somewhere new to live, I decided to post a personal ad at the same time. I wrote something like:

I'm a lesbian who is over dating. I am looking for someone to cuddle with. Serious responses only. Please don't respond if you are a guy or looking for sex.

After posting the Craigslist ad, I got a few sleazy responses, but one response looked promising. One "lesbian" (as he self-identified at the time) appeared like a good fit for what I was looking for. That person would turn out to be Jay.

Jay sounded fun and kind, interested in cuddling, and worked at a bookstore. Unfortunately for me, Jay's response was all written in all lowercase letters. The lack of capitalization reminded me of my middle school students. All day long at work, I am telling students to start their sentences with a capital letter. I almost didn't write back to Jay because of his lack of capitalization, which seems really silly in retrospect.

But...he seemed like the most promising person by far —and the only one I was really interested in—so I wasn't going to let capital letters get in the way of cuddling. (Turns out Jay was an English major and is much more proficient in grammar than I am! He was not capitalizing on purpose! And now when I have something important to write, he frequently edits my writing.)

Jay had left his number in the response. I called him up, and we decided to give cuddling a try. Though, it would be a few weeks until the timing worked out for both of us. I was leaving on vacation to San Diego over part of the school winter break. We decided to meet up after I returned from my trip. Jay would come to my co-op. That way, we could cuddle that night if we both felt comfortable with each other. I figured with all my roommates, someone else would be around. But I didn't realize other people were traveling during their winter vacations as well.

We were supposed to meet an hour after I returned from the airport. Less than five minutes after our arranged meeting time, when he hadn't arrived, I called to make sure he was actually showing up.

Jay was already parked around the corner, but when he

answered the call, he told me he was parking and would be there soon. A few minutes later, he bounded up the stairs as promised.

Jay wore an orange shirt with a waffle weave. He had on baggy jeans. Though he was presenting as female at the time, he had a soft butch look to him. He had a shaved head and was the most beautiful person I had ever seen. I still can imagine him through the window, and I still remember the jolt that went through me at first sight. I'd never believed in that "love at first sight" thing. Maybe it was more like "lust at first sight," but whatever it was, the feeling was powerful.

We sat on one of the overstuffed couches in the co-op living room and chatted. We had tea. Of course, we had tea —fabulous lesbians that we were! We were both nervous, which meant Jay asked me lots of questions and I talked a lot. He asked me about my job. I pulled out my actual curriculum planning books and showed him how I taught seventh grade math.

Jay listened attentively. Sometime later, we agreed we felt comfortable with the idea of cuddling that night. Jay had a prepared overnight bag in his car, so he retrieved that.

After Jay returned, I asked him if he wanted to go in the hot tub. I find, to this day, taking a hot bath or getting in a hot tub helps me fall asleep faster. The heat, followed by the cooler temperature of the bed, is a soothing combination for me.

He replied something to the effect of, "But I don't have a swimsuit." To which I replied, "Oh, that's not a problem.

We don't need to use swimsuits here at the co-op." I meant nothing other than what I said. I tend to be very literal and say what I mean. I also tend to assume everyone else means exactly what they say, no more, no less. In retrospect, I can see Jay probably thought I was coming onto him or sending a sign, but I was oblivious to the possible message.

Behind the house was the hot tub. Walking out back, it seemed as if we were transported to another time and place. There were giant eucalyptus plants wafting their sweet scent and lots of other green shrubs and plants. That night there were tons of stars. It was silent and beautiful.

I didn't know that Jay is practically blind without glasses. The hot tub fogged them up, so he took them off and continued to pretend to go along with me as I pointed out the big dipper. Even though he couldn't see the stars that night, it is still a special memory for both of us—the humor and the meaning, and why we eventually designed our own wedding rings with the big dipper on them. But we "looked" at a few other constellations and then both got too hot and decided it was time for bed and cuddling.

We wrapped towels around ourselves, feeling a bit self-conscious and careful to not look at each other. We dried off, dressed in our jammies, brushed our teeth, and climbed into bed.

At first, we cuddled. I was the little spoon, and Jay the big spoon. Then that became too hot, so we switched. Jay was the little spoon, and I became the big spoon. Then we turned back over, and I became the little spoon. Jay's hand snuggled against my stomach and we both tried to sleep. I slowed my breathing and tried to relax.

This was not quite like I had imagined. Somehow this wasn't the peaceful drifting off to sleep experience I expected.

Here was this very real, beautiful, attentive body pressed against mine. Meanwhile, Jay realized at some point that there was no way to move his arm or hand without looking like he was making a move on me. Move his hand up from my stomach, and it would appear like he was reaching toward my boobs. Move his hand down, or even slightly move to adjust, and it would appear like he was reaching elsewhere. In the meantime, I felt my heartbeat racing. I tried to control my breathing, but I couldn't control that any more than my heartbeat. I was probably breathing at a normal rate, but I suddenly was very aware of each inhale and exhale.

It became clear that maybe something more would be ok with both of us. I don't remember quite how that conversation went, but one way or another, we managed to communicate consent to each other.

In the end, not too much sleep happened that night. The next morning, around 6 am, we both woke up. Jay went to the bathroom and was shocked by what he saw. I accidentally gave him a ring of hickeys. Not one or two, but a whole cascade of them. I was extremely embarrassed. I didn't realize that could happen so easily on his skin, or that I had gotten so carried away! I had definitely never given someone a hickey before and felt embarrassed.

Not really believing that we had actually slept together,

I tried to rush him out of the co-op before my roommates came home. I quickly scrambled him eggs and hurried him out of the co-op. I thought, okay, that was an amazing one-night stand, but I would probably never see him again. Except I didn't stop thinking about him.

Jay was such an attentive listener. I felt like we connected, and I had clicked with him. Did he feel the same way?

A week later, I called Jay to find out if he might be interested in going out on a real date. We could do a do-over. After dating for a while, we both agreed to become exclusive.

And that was, of course, just the beginning of a tremendous adventure that would become our life together.

Part II

February Present Day

Now, eighteen years later, we would celebrate a new first Valentine's Day.

Our first holiday with both Jay and me knowing that he was actually a trans guy. It would be our first holiday with family traditions after Jay transitioned.

Since having three children (Cole, Liz and Joan), Valentine's Day has morphed into this day to celebrate both our love, but also our family. It was and is a special family day for all of us. Every year Jay got little (or big) bags for the kids with toys and chocolates, and we always make nice cards. Many years we made homemade heart shaped mini pizzas.

On our first Valentine's Day post-realization, I put on a new pink sweatshirt with a slight turtleneck. The inside felt fuzzy and the outside smooth. It was my idea of sensory heaven. The previous day I got a haircut, so my hair was shoulder length. I put on some lipstick (not normal for me at all!) and walked downstairs to a beautiful sight.

Walking into our kitchen, I saw a table full of four piles of presents. Each of our children had a stuffed animal, hearts, and a bag of chocolate. There was a gift bag for me as well. Jay made us a nice breakfast and before leaving for school, Cole, our oldest child, agreed to take a photo with Jay and me. I admire those pictures to this day of both Jay and me. We looked radiant. (If I may say so. And since I'm writing. I say so!)

I told everyone I loved them and headed out to work. Midway through teaching one of my morning classes, I got a call from the office saying there was a delivery for me. This was shocking for me. I didn't think I had ever had a delivery at work before.

Someone walked down from the office carrying a vase of flowers, a helium balloon that said, "I love you," and a card. What an incredible surprise. I smiled from ear to ear, totally overwhelmed with love.

After school, I went home and hung out with the family. Jay and I don't always go out on the actual Valentine's Day. Usually we wait for the weekend, but this particular year we did. Jay seemed a bit out of sorts at dinner, so I asked him what was up. Turns out, he had unexpectedly come out to both of his parents. While they took it as well as expected—no one expects to have that conversation, and I really can't imagine how that was for them—Jay coming out was not something his parents suspected. It was a tremendous surprise to them, coming out from left field, and beyond shocking.

Jay was buzzing with anxious energy from that conversation. He was so raw that he had what we call a vulnerability hangover. That is when one's nerves are so raw from an interaction that everything feels off. His heart was beating fast, noises felt louder than they were, and everything overwhelmed him.

The restaurant we went to was extremely busy. (It was Valentine's Day after all.) We were seated in the middle of the room, and it was just all too much. It wasn't the romantic, quiet dinner either of us hoped the night would be. I wanted the evening to feel special, but I was putting too much pressure on the night out. I also felt protective of Jay's feelings from the experience.

Of course, neither of us expected he would come out that day. The opportunity presented itself and he took the chance to be more fully himself. I was both proud of him and selfishly disappointed about how the day ended. Which then I felt guilty for being self-centered. Underneath everything, I knew it was just one of many dinners and it did not have to be perfect.

After Valentine's Day, the pace of coming out accelerated. Over the course of two weeks, Jay figured out his name. We came out to the children, the children's biological father, and my parents. I also met a couple that would become mentors for me, where one spouse transitioned after they had children. To top it off, we also got a new puppy. And we gave away Jay's old clothes.

It was a cascade of changes.

We just took one moment at a time.

Jay and I knew he needed a new name. His birth name sounded feminine and wouldn't be able to stay with him through the transition. His old name was one that his parents loved. In particular, his mom really loved the old name and seemed to enjoy sharing about how they had come up with the unique spelling. So, it would not be an easy name to change.

First, we thought about the alternate names that Jay's parents had considered if he "had been born a boy." That name really didn't fit him. Plus, their first choice was the name of a boy who bullied me relentlessly when I was a teenager and made me cry on a regular basis for multiple years.

When we were pregnant with our children (Jay with Cole and me with Liz and Joan), we had looked at a baby name book. We made a list of the names we liked and then tried a name out. It wasn't until we tried out a name that we knew it was the right one. Of course, it is possible the children will want to change their names in the future, which will be fine.

We took that same approach with Jay's new name. We found a different name and tried it. We couldn't use the name during the day when the kids were around. They didn't know anything was going on. (Even though Liz overheard part of that first conversation after the hot tub, she never brought it up again and actually seemed to forget it completely.) But after they went to bed each night, we tried out a new name. One of the first names we tried for a few weeks was Adam. That name just didn't feel right to either of us, in the end.

After a week or two, Jay sat down and looked at all the letters in his old first and middle name. Jay has always liked crossword puzzles and other challenges with words. I'm much more of a Sudoku and KenKen type of solver. I've never solved a large crossword puzzle in my life. But Jay loves that type of challenge.

Moving all the letters around, he came up with a new first name. The letters were in his old two names. I think there is some nice symbolism there, metamorphosing the old name into a new name and future.

For his middle name, I think the choice was easy. When we were first married (the first of 5 marriages/commitment ceremonies trying to legally tie the knot) we changed our last names to be hyphenated. But that turned out not to work so well. Just the way our names sound when they are hyphenated caused confusion for people. The last straw was on our babymoon. We went to San Diego and purchased tickets to go to Sea World. The tickets were supposed to be at the entrance with a Southwest Airlines vacation package. They tried a million different combinations but couldn't find any tickets for us. Finally, it turned out they had confused our hyphenated name for a first and last name. We decided we didn't want our child to have this challenge, along with the other challenges of having two moms. So, some point after that, we dropped the hyphenated name and changed our names again. This was the second legal name change we did.

Jay decided he wanted to take his old last name and

make that his new middle name. It was like the hyphenated name, but in reverse! It would be his third and hopefully final name change. When Jay suggested his new name, I felt tingles. I felt chills right in my heart. The previous name he had tried didn't give me that type of emotional response.

I knew we had a keeper. This was his new name.

Meanwhile, we were still using his old name and pronouns during the day. But once the kids went to bed, around 8 pm most nights, we would move to his new name and pronoun. I wanted to be prepared to use his new name (without too many mistakes!) once we came out to the kids. So, as I drove to and from work every day in the car, I would practice using it out loud. I'd pretend to have spoken conversations using his name and pronouns. I'm sure it looked like I was talking on a hands-free device, but really I was talking out loud to myself.

This wasn't a totally new thing for me. I often practiced conversations in the car. On my way to work on Mondays, I often thought about and practiced my answer to, "How was your weekend?" Don't ask me why, but that is a stressful question for me. Since I know people are going to ask me how my weekend was, I come up with a response ahead of time.

Jay was one of the few people I had never rehearsed for our conversations. His transition, however, led me to practice and rehearse for what our future conversations would be like. I wanted to be used to the changes before they became our reality.

Driving to and from work, I would say all sorts of

things out loud, such as table manners. "Jay, will you pass the salt?" I would practice phrases like this or sentences I might say to other people about Jay. For example, I would practice saying, "Jay took Tango out for a walk. <u>He</u> will be back in a few minutes." I made sure to practice his pronoun too! "<u>He</u> is at the store getting groceries."

It felt really strange at first. What I found deeply unsettling was that it felt like I was talking about someone else. Not my love and spouse. Even though I had that initial tingling feeling with his name, I didn't have the emotional connection with it.

I also missed the old name. That was the name of the person I had fallen in love with, married to a few times, done second-parent adoptions with, bought our first house with and so many other firsts.

Then in my therapy group I had more opportunities to practice saying his new name around other people and talk with his pronouns. It turns out you don't really use a person's pronouns that much when you are talking to them directly with no one else around. So outside of my imaginary conversations, it was helpful to have a place where I could practice for real.

Also, to help me with the new name, I was using his new name in my phone. This meant every time he called, my phone screen would show his new name. For a long time, when I would use the dial assist in the car, I would accidentally say his old name or be confused about where his name had gone. Then I would remember, "Oh, he changed his name," and then make the call.

One of my past fears with his new name was that I

would use his old name when we were being intimate together. I was afraid that I would use the previous name unconsciously and hurt his feelings. I don't recall slipping up then, but even if I had, it wouldn't have been the end of the world.

Interestingly, once Jay came out and shared his name with other people, they seemed to suddenly remember his name. Previously, people had a really hard time remembering his name. I have since wondered if there was something about the name that didn't match with who he really was at a soul level.

Practicing Pronouns

Recently I talked with someone who I hadn't seen in years. They asked how Jay was doing, but used his old name, which honestly sounded strange to my ears. Even though that was the name I used for 18 years, I no longer associate it with him. But slip ups are to be expected, and it's best to plan ahead for them. Slip-ups now are

Part II

extremely rare and are a distant echo of those initial years.

For me, the most likely times to slip up were when I was exhausted, concentrating on something else, or when I was indirectly interacting with Jay. I learned with time to not make a big deal about it. I just corrected myself and moved on. I often felt embarrassed, but I learned that over-apologizing actually made things worse for Jay.

In the beginning of Jay's transition, my brain had 18 years of neural pathways using the pronoun "she". Those neural pathways were so strong because they involved falling in love, having children, and many other special moments. These emotions made our neural pathways strong, but now, many years of new emotions have rewritten those old pathways.

As strange as this sounds, it really helped to have conversations in the car with myself, practicing sentences out loud using his correct pronoun. Why is it important to practice out loud? For me, it is crucial to practice the same way you will use the skill in real life. Imagine trying to shoot a basketball by only visualizing shooting it. That might help a bit, but you also have to practice the actual shooting to really improve. In the car, I would practice sentences to build up those new pathways faster, stronger, and smoother than they would naturally. I would say things like, "Can you pass the salt to him?" "He is in the kitchen." "He is going for a run."

About a year or two after his transition, I started having moments where I worried that I had mis-gendered other people and would second guess myself. *Did I use the right pronoun?* This concern passed with time, and now I don't think much about pronoun usage, unless I'm around people who still haven't built up their new pathways.

∼

So, we had Jay's new name settled. He had bravely come out to his parents. Now, we were ready for the next set of challenges: coming out to more people. We needed to come out to my parents and our three children. We also needed to come out to our dear friend and the biological father of our three children.

We were both a little apprehensive about how the children were going to take the news. When Liz heard Jay say he "might not be a woman," after coming in from the hot tub in December, she insisted there was no way that could be true. "Mama, you're a lady," she had emphatically responded.

Our youngest, Joan, liked her routines. She would get extremely upset if we changed the order of her morning, didn't play her preferred music in the car, or asked her to wear a coat outside because it was raining. She has autism, though we didn't know it at the time. Changing small things in her daily life causes her significant stress. Jay coming out as trans, changing his name and pronouns would not be a small change, and so we were not sure how she would take that news.

Liz we were less concerned about. Even though she had initially gotten upset when Jay said maybe he was not a woman, she generally is easy going and we thought it would be fine after the adjustment period.

Cole was a wild card in our minds. He was in middle school and very close to both Jay and me. We just had no clue about how he would respond.

I started by doing some research. Unfortunately, I couldn't find any decent advice online about how to come out to one's children. So I asked people in my therapy group and received some suggestions. First, people said that we should tell them together. That would help the children feel supported. Second, people suggested Jay leave after coming out so the children could ask me any questions they might have. Next, they suggested it was important we emphasize we were staying together. Finally, the group suggested we buy some children's books that introduced the idea of transness.

Jay and I had the book *Red: A Crayon's Story* by Michael Hall. This is a book about a crayon who has the label blue written on it but is really a red crayon. Every time the crayon tries to draw something blue, it comes out as red. The crayon keeps on getting upset until it realizes that the label on the crayon was wrong. The children had heard the book before, but we read it a few more times before the day of coming out. Then we planned our coming out evening for the kids. Jay would go to a support group for people who had newly come out as trans later in the evening, so we decided that would be the perfect evening to share the news.

I'm not sure how or why, but the three kids, Jay and I, ended up in Cole's room in the early evening. Sitting down on the bed, Jay shared we had something to talk about with them. I don't remember this conversation too clearly, so this is the best I can recollect. I think I started by saying, "We have something to share with you."

Feeling really nervous about how this was going, I looked over at Jay. He, most likely feeling apprehensive about how this would go, told the kids. "I've recently realized that I'm transgender. And we wanted to let you know."

The kids had a moment of quiet. Then Liz asked a question. "You're gay. So... you and Mommy?"

I realized quickly what Liz was asking. Were we breaking up? If Jay was gay, and I was a lesbian and he transitioned, then clearly, we would separate. Concerned that we were causing unnecessary stress, I quickly assured them we were still married, and nothing was going to change that. They all had a few more questions, which led to their most important question: "Will you get married again? And if you do get married again, can we ride in a zebra limousine to the party?" Once Liz said that, I knew we were in the clear.

A few years earlier, for our tenth anniversary, we were finally legally married. We had rented a zebra limousine to take us to a state that allowed gay marriage. While in the limousine, our minister folded a turkey out of a towel. The fancy wheels, the amazing towel origami, and snazzy clothes are all highlights. The kids let me know that there was a rainbow light disco in the panel that divided the

Part II

front from the back, and they didn't need to wear seat belts. So, they had highlights of their own. Of course, getting an actual legal marriage certificate was THE highlight of the day! After 10 years and multiple attempts at marriage, that legal piece of paper felt like pure gold.

After Jay came out, the kids wanted to know if we could do a zebra limousine again. As of yet, we haven't done that, but one never knows. At the time, I truthfully said, "I don't know. We will see. But that would be really fun." I knew once we moved onto talking about the white and black striped wheels, the kids were done with the initial big questions. It was time for some laughter and fun.

And really, coming out was so much more challenging in my head than it was in real life. The kids were alright. While there would be more questions to come and more conversations as Jay came out to wider and wider circles of people, our immediate family was all on board with supporting him.

Around that same time, we shared an email with my parents explaining the situation. They responded quickly that they were excited to have a new son in the family. My parents were really supportive of both of us and just wanted to make sure I was ok.

That was a tremendous relief, even though getting there was extremely challenging. Coming out was emotionally draining for both of us, though of course much more so for Jay. Each time he would have a vulnerability hangover.

Meanwhile, I felt this powerful need to show a united

front and be 100% supportive. But I also had a firm belief I needed to fully mask my wider range of emotions. I was afraid if people knew the range of how this was affecting me, they would be less supportive of Jay and our family. I wanted his family and my parents and our children to be protected from the fuller range of my experience. But this meant very few people understood what I was going through. I am a private person to begin with, but having a few friends I could really talk with and a therapy group to attend were lifesavers for me.

I was stressed, masking my full range of emotions around my family. Jay was still vulnerable and raw. Incredible changes kept on happening. I felt like we needed some lightness and joy. How that joy came into our life continues to surprise me to this day.

The Friday after Valentine's Day, Liz was invited to a sleepover at a friend's house. I drove the following morning to pick her up, arriving early and listening to "Cake by the Ocean" on full blast in the car. I sat in the car for a few minutes while a sense of inspiration and sparkles came to me in a simple thought.

We should get a dog.

What?? I thought, wondering if I had heard that right. But then the original thought settled around me.

A dog?

We had one dog already. And in all honesty, I was lukewarm about getting that dog. It took years of convincing, a pro/con list, and more than one family meeting before I agreed. After the first dog, Jay would talk about getting another one for Tango to play with. I had been dead set against getting another dog every time he brought it up.

Really? A dog?

I continued to listen to "Cake by the Ocean" and when the time was right, walked over to the door to pick up Liz. Then, when I entered the house, they had this very cute dog. It was so cuddly and fabulous. I gave the dog some pets and felt a sense of peace wash over me.

Another thought came to me.

This is exactly what we need. A puppy would bring us so much joy and love and would be something other than Jay's transition to focus on. This might be a good thing.

However, another part of me thought the idea was totally crazy. How was this a good time to bring more chaos into our family? But I told that doubting part of myself to just take a little rest and asked the rest of my mind to stay curious.

Liz said goodbye to her friends, and we drove home.

Walking in the door, we both slipped off our shoes. We walked past the laundry room, and I said hi to Jay in our office.

After greeting Liz, he looked at me with a twinkle in his eyes, "Come take a look at this." He held out his phone to me. I walked a little closer and peered at the screen.

"Look at this. Tango (our dog) has a niece. Are you sure you don't want another puppy?" And he looked at me with these huge innocent eyes.

Jay then showed me this very cute video of a puppy running and playing in a field. It was a very little black puppy with a white spot under its chin, just like Tango. It was bounding with joy and energy and looked so happy.

The coincidence wasn't lost on me. *Okay, I get it.* I thought to myself. But I wasn't about to tell Jay. Then another idea came to me. *What if I surprise him with a puppy?*

More than once, Jay had mentioned that one thing he wanted sometimes during his life was to be surprised with a puppy for Christmas. *He will never in a million years suspect this. It would be perfect.*

To Jay I said, "You know I don't want another dog. One is enough."

"I know, I know." Jay said, dropping it immediately.

Meanwhile, I walked upstairs and did a quick internet search for the dog Jay had showed me. The dog was totally adorable and listed as still available. While part of me thought *this was totally crazy*, I decided *I'm going for this.*

Not putting it off, I closed the door to our bedroom. Standing as far as I could from the door, I called the dog breeder. They had a place on the beach, which was a solid five-hour drive from our house. I had no clue how I would pull this off, but I called anyway.

We chatted briefly about how well Tango was doing and then I asked, "Is the adorable black puppy still available? What is her personality like?"

The breeder shared the puppy was an incredibly sweet dog and playful but also cuddly.

I decided we should go for it and secretly planned the entire trip.

The breeder and I set everything up so Jay and I would

drive down to get the puppy the following week during the school day. I would take the day off from work and they would meet us about two hours from our home.

While it was challenging enough for us to have one dog, two guinea pigs, three cats and a fish, how much more work could another dog be? Part of me thought getting another dog on top of that seemed totally insane. But I trusted all the signs and my intuition. Maybe this is just what we all needed?

Maybe the dog would be good for me, too.

I really like training dogs. When we got Tango, I enjoyed teaching her to sit and be calm and playing with her. I might not be the most consistent with taking walks, but I love teaching dogs new skills. When I was training Tango, I didn't think about other things. It was just me and the dog. I watched lots of videos. With some help, she got good at shaking, spinning, and high-fiving. I figured that having a second dog couldn't be that much more difficult. It would be the same number of walks and everything.

Fast forward a week. I told Jay I had a big surprise for him and we needed to clean up the house to be ready for the surprise. The kids helped, and we all cleaned the place together.

The day of the big surprise, we woke up to snow outside. It was heavy enough that school was canceled.

I was concerned we wouldn't be able to get out of our neighborhood and onto the main roads because we have a steep hill to access the main roads. Thankfully, though, that wasn't a problem.

I piled the kids and Jay in the car and told them we had

a few hours to drive for our surprise. While in the driveway, they peppered me with questions and asked for the millionth time what we were getting.

I convinced them, rather briefly, that I was getting them a rat! Turns out no one was excited about a rat! I learned quickly that Jay and Joan both hate rats. (Liz, Cole, and I all had a good laugh out of that, though.)

Once we reached the top of the neighborhood, it was clear driving from there. There was a bit of snow, but not too bad. The freeways were totally fine. We listened to music and drove along down I-5 to our destination and stopped at a Subway to wait. Before buying sandwiches, I asked everyone to take a final guess on the surprise.

Cole's guesses included a new carpet and a boat. Jay thought we were getting a robot vacuum cleaner and Liz was stuck with the idea that I was actually getting them a rat.

From an actual video from the day:

Me: What do you think the surprise is?

Cole: I thought it was a boat at first. No. I thought it was a carpet at first. Because.

Me: Because you had to clear the carpet.

Cole: Yeah. Because we had to clear the carpet. But then I thought it was a rat. Because animals need space. Then I thought. Now I think it's a boat. But carpet is probably the best guess.

Part II

Me to Jay: How are you feeling right now?

Jay: I'm excited to find out what the surprise is.

Me: Any ideas yet?

Jay: There have been lots of guesses.

Joan: Like a kitty cat.

Liz: A rat.

Joan: A robot vacuum.

Jay: Carpet.

Cole: Mama's was the robot vacuum.

Jay: Rumba. Joan says she guessed it first.

Me: Well, we will see.

We all get out of the car and carefully walk through the snow toward an aqua blue pickup truck. Cole leading the pack, followed by Liz. Joan held Jay's hand so she wouldn't slip and fall in the snow.

Jay: Ohhh????

Joan (confused): Is that Tango????? (The name of our other dog.)

Jay: Oh my god. Oh My god. You got us a dog?

Liz: You mean you bought us another dog?

Me: It is the one you chose.

Jay: Yah.

Liz: You got us another dog? What????

Liz clapped her hands and danced in a circle on the ground.

Jay introduced himself with his new name... for the first time with someone outside of our family.

After the initial meet and greet of our small, new puppy, and the surprise and shock that "Mom actually got us a puppy," we trundled back into the car for the two-hour drive home.

Quickly, the topic of deciding a name for the puppy came up. While Jay had a new name, our puppy did not. While driving home, we all agreed we would wait a full week before naming our new puppy. We would try out a few different names to see how they sounded. (Sound familiar?)

Name or not, everyone wanted to hold the puppy all at

Part II

the same time. Even though we had plenty of time for everyone to take a turn, it was difficult to decide who would go first or how long each person would get. To prevent massive squabbling, I set my phone timer for ten minutes and let the kids know we would rotate puppy holding time. This way, everyone would have plenty of turns.

The puppy cuddled with each child, one at a time. Snuggled on their chest with a fuzzy red blanket, the puppy became everyone's focus. Every time the timer went off, we rotated. The timer worked perfectly.

Jay couldn't stop smiling. Every so often he would exclaim, "I can't believe you got us a dog. I totally can't believe it. And the dog that I chose!" His face was alive with joy.

I had wondered more than once in the week between the phone call and the drive if I was completely and utterly out of my mind. Having a new puppy is a lot of work. I had wondered if this was the best time to bring that extra burden into our lives? The answer turned out to be a resounding yes! Bringing a new dog into the family wasn't such a crazy idea, after all.

"What about Curly? What about Pepper?" Lots of names were thrown out into the air.

Liz said, "What about Bubbles? I think we should name her Bubbles."

I reminded them that testing out all names was fine, but we wouldn't be making a choice for a week unless everyone agreed.

Part way back to our house, our minivan needed gas.

Jay suggested we stop at a gas station, get some snacks, and use the bathroom. Jay and the kids piled out of the van, and I finally got my very first chance to hold this new puppy. With her cuddled in my lap, I felt a deep calm spread through me. Her fur felt like velvet as I nuzzled into this newest edition of our family and enjoyed a moment of silence in the car with her. The minutes were oh, so sweet and way too short.

Soon everyone returned, eager to resume their puppy-holding time, but Jay stated, "It was Mommy's idea to get us the puppy. She should get a few minutes with her, too." He suggested everyone should watch the Mr. Rogers video we had on the DVD player.

When we turned it on, it was at the end of an episode about bubbles. Mr. Rogers played the piano keys while talking about the amazing and fabulous world of bubbles.

Bubbles? I thought. *Hmm . . .*

"Bubbles! Bubbles!" cried Liz from the back of the car. "See. Mr. Rogers said Bubbles! Did you hear that? We HAVE to name our new dog Bubbles."

Amazingly, everyone agreed.

So, less than two hours after meeting our puppy, she had a name. Turns out we didn't need a week or any big family meeting to come to a consensus.

Bubbles had come into our life. When we got home, Jay and I looked at the adoption certificate. Jay quickly said, "Look at this. Bubble's birthday is the day the kid's great grandma would have turned 100." It seemed like one more sign that Bubbles was sent here for a reason and was

Part II

almost like Jay's grandma came into our house to help us out during this transition, at least in spirit.

Bubbles turned out to be the playful, yet calm, loving puppy we all needed during this time of change. Just like iridescent soap bubbles that we love blowing during the summer, Bubbles brought infectious joy and beauty into our life.

The next discussion became where would Bubbles sleep at night? We created a rotation schedule, but Bubbles would get one night with Jay and me first. She was Jay's coming out puppy after all! Bubbles would then rotate between the children's rooms each night. At least, that was the plan.

Bubbles settled into our household. We now had two dogs, three cats, a betta fish, and two guinea pigs. Who needs a zoo membership when you have a zoo in the house?

Everyone enjoyed playing and cuddling with Bubbles, which, true to her name, had a light, playful personality. Easy going, she loved to snuggle and continues to this day to be a bundle of joy.

In our family, we now say, when you come out as gay, you get a toaster. But when you come out as trans, you get a puppy! (Interestingly, the Ellen DeGeneres episode where she comes out is titled "The Puppy Episode." I hadn't made the connection until writing this book, but she was certainly onto something. The title was used as a code name prior to her coming out.)

After clearing out space to get ready for the new puppy, Jay and I continued to be on a cleaning and resetting kick. At the end of February, we tackled our clothes. We had been watching a Netflix documentary on the Marie Kondo method for cleaning, which is intense. We committed to using the Marie Kondo method for just our clothes. If Jay was getting a wardrobe makeover, I could too! The basic method is that we made an enormous pile of clothes, shoes, scarfs, belts, socks, underwear. Everything.

Why go small when you can go big?

I piled all the clothes on the bed and just stared at this heap of belongings, all our clothing in one place! Once we had a humongous pile, we went through one item at a time. I would ask myself, "Does this spark joy?" If the answer was yes, I put it in a keeping pile. If the answer was no, I thanked the item for being part of my life and put it in the giveaway pile.

I held each piece of clothing in my hands before deciding. I found it easy to see which pieces I liked and which I didn't. Jay coming out as trans helped me rethink and reevaluate my own style. It turns out that even though I am not a traditional girly girl, occasionally I do like lace, sparkles, and flowers and twirly dresses! Typically, I prefer jeans and a t-shirt, and I almost never wear make-up. My only jewelry is my wedding ring, engagement ring, elastic bracelets, and a sentimental necklace.

Clothing items that were plain rarely sparked a sense of joy. I think they were clothes I thought I should wear to look presentable. There were additional pieces of clothes that I had been holding onto, but when I looked at them, it was clear they were worn out. I could see the cotton was pilling up and pants that had been washed too many times. For these clothes, I said thank you and added them to the outgoing pile.

As Jay and I tackled our piles, I encountered some of his old clothes in my stack. At some point in our relationship, our clothes migrated from one side of the closet to the other. They were clothes that Jay would never wear now, but he had worn in the past before coming out as trans. I had no way of knowing how much they did not spark joy for him. He was wearing them just to be "presentable" and mask his true feelings.

There was this one tunic sweater with stripes of different shades of tan and white. It wasn't particularly feminine (in my mind at the time), but I liked the way Jay looked when he wore it. He normally wore it over leggings and looked amazing. But I just didn't realize how uncomfortable it made him. Of course, now, looking back, I see things differently.

As I held that sweater in my hand, a wave of grief and sadness poured over me. I sat down on the floor, looking at this beautiful tan and white sweater that he would never wear again, and felt a profound loss. Loss that I would never see Jay wearing this anymore. We would never go on a date with him wearing this again.

I said thank you to the sweater. Held it up to my face and folded it with love. And then, with tears in my eyes, I placed it into the pile to give away. Eventually, the grief passed, but I let it take its course.

Before learning Jay was trans, and before getting counseling in the spouse's group, I would have tried to push away my grief. I never would have sat with those feelings like I had with this sweater. I would have ignored them, made myself busy, denied them, stuffing them down, down, down in my throat and heart. I would not have been aware of avoiding the painful emotions. But the therapy group helped me learn to sit with uncomfortable feelings, learning they would not last forever.

I said goodbye to the sweater and to that tiny memory of Jay from the past.

Being able to say goodbye to his clothes somehow also helped me honor and say goodbye to the old appearance of him. I could thank the clothes for the wonderful memories we shared and for being in my life. There was something cathartic about holding each item in my hands and saying goodbye.

I continued to sort my clothes. Less than five minutes later, I held up a jacket to Jay and asked if this had been his. He said yes. It was from our legal marriage. I was shocked that I didn't remember he had worn the jacket to our wedding. (I guess when one has 5 ceremonies, events, etc., the clothing blurs together.)

Suddenly, more waves of emotion poured through me again. I felt joy for the wedding, and a profound sense of loss. I was no longer married to a woman. After we fought so hard to get married, I was now no longer married to a woman.

I didn't want to lose this memory or piece of our history. I teared up and said, "I don't think I can let this go."

Jay replied, "You don't have to say goodbye to it. There is no rush. It's Okay."

I took the black jacket, folded it, and put it in the keep pile—*my* keep pile. Even though I would never wear it, I wasn't ready to let it go.

Later that night, I couldn't fall asleep. The day's emotions wired me. I felt both energized and unsettled. I decided that meditating and having some pot was exactly what I needed. Maybe some herbal medicine would help me see this day in a new way, or at least fall asleep.

Quietly, I tiptoed out of our bedroom. He mumbled that he heard me, rolled over, and fell back into rhythmic breathing.

I walked down the stairs, through the laundry room, and opened the door to the garage. I shimmied past the car and freezer and out the back door. I stood outside for a moment. The clouds covered the stars, and there were no leaves on the trees. It was quite calm. The air was cool and still. I sat at the back of our garage, looking at our rhododendron bush. The buds looked ready to bloom, even though that was months away. The grass was muddy and full of winter rain.

First, I took some deep breaths to clear my mind. Breathing deeply in and out, I calmed myself and felt rooted to the Earth. I imagined roots flowing from my feet, grounding me all the way to the core of the earth. I imagined light pouring in through the sky, coming down through the crown of my head. I just sat with the presence of the night sky.

Once I was ready, I took in some herbal medicine. I

paused for a moment, and then slowly let it out. After a bit, I put everything back safe from children.

It was time to meditate.

One of my favorite ways to meditate to this day is in water. I went out to the hot tub—the very place Jay had his epiphany. I laid down in the water and put a floating pillow under my head so I could relax as much as possible. While floating, I slowly felt peaceful and connected to that which is bigger than me.

I focused on my breath. Breathing in and out in a rhythm. In two, out two. In two, out two. Over and over, I breathed. I relaxed my body and let the water carry all my weight. I released and relaxed as much as possible. I meditated in silence for a long time, releasing all the emotions, thoughts, and excitement of the day.

Then, suddenly, I had a moment of clarity.

A voice in my head said, "None of the clothes we gave away today were the clothes Jay wore when you met him." I remembered that when we met, he had a much more androgynous style prior to becoming a "mom" and listening to his inner voice about how he was "supposed" to dress in that role.

I sat with that.

It was just one simple thought. Then silence again.

I felt a lightness bubble up in my heart.

Oh. I realized at that moment I was holding on to the material as if they were Jay. But Jay isn't his clothes. Jay isn't what he wears. Jay isn't even what he looks like. He is deeper than that. Jay is the spirit deep within that resides in this physical body. That isn't changing. I fell in love with his spirit and soul, not his clothes.

I sat with that idea and floated, letting peace flow through me.

More thoughts followed that sense of peace and acceptance. *I really do love Jay in his new clothes*. I rested in that thought for a while.

Then another idea came to me.

I actually love his new clothes. He is so attractive and fabulous in his button up shirts and new jeans. He has a more relaxed look about him. He is clearly more at home and comfortable, and that confidence and joy are gorgeous.

From there, I went back into a space of meditation. At some point, I had to pee. Laughing, I thought, well, the physical real world gave me a sign that it was time to end my meditation and go to bed.

I went upstairs after my meditation, feeling so much lighter. I fell asleep and woke up the next day full of peace and acceptance for whatever change came next.

Chapter 5

March

We had one new dog, two new names, and a whole lot of puppy energy in the house. But all that excitement was just the beginning.

Jay was one month out from starting testosterone (T). And in just a few weeks, we would come out to everyone we saw on a regular basis. That included all the parents in all three children's classes and colleagues at work. We just needed to figure out when and how to do this. Being upfront about who we are is important to both of us.

Before sharing our approach to coming out with you, I think it is important to understand who we were before he transitioned. We lived as an openly lesbian couple. Even though we live in the suburbs, for most of the last decade we were out to our neighbors and colleagues at work and parents at our children's school.

Particularly as a teacher, I made it a point to come out. I have taught every grade from K-8. It wasn't always easy to be out, but over time, it became easier. I know it made a big difference to students who had queer parents themselves or would go onto identify that way themselves. During the first few years at my last school, as I walked down the hallway, some students would say things like "That's so gay" when they meant something was stupid. That made me cringe. I know it wasn't about me, but I still don't enjoy hearing it. Not only that, but what about other kids who are gay? They shouldn't have to hear homophobic statements while studying reading, writing, and arithmetic.

I made it a point to stop the middle school students to inform them that homophobic language is not tolerated at school. I would say, "What's wrong with being gay? That's really not okay to say." Slowly, students stopped saying homophobic words where I could hear.

Inside my own classroom, I never heard homophobic language. I made it a point to come out on the first day of school as part of my meet and greet first hour of class. On the first day, I always did a slide show so the students would get to know me. I normally set up some math problems, and the answer gave students information about me.

For example, I might post the problem: 10 + 9 - 11 = ?

Once the students calculate the answer, I show the next slide. On that slide, it has the number eight for the answer, along with pictures of the eight animals we have in our house. (Yes, at the time we had eight animals!)

"We have eight animals in my house. Here is a picture of our three cats, two guinea pigs, two fish and one dog. I really love animals. Talk to your neighbor and ask what is your favorite animal, and why?"

After a few more problems, I would come out to my students in the form of a math problem.

"I have 30 seeds. I have six pots. How many seeds should I place in each pot if I want to use all the seeds?"

I would pop up the next slide: "This is my family. I live with five people, including me. These are my three children. Cole is 10 years old, Liz is 9 years old and Joan is 6 years old and this is my wife. Cole loves building with Legos and Liz is flexible and enjoys tumbling. Joan is a big fan of listening to music and swinging."

And just like that, I'd come out to my students. I purposely come out in a way that is like how straight teachers come out. I adapted my Google slide presentation from another teacher in our building. Straight teachers come out on their first day too, as easily as showing a picture of their husband or wife and children. Most straight teachers have many pictures of their families around their desks. So, I did the same thing.

Was I nervous the first year I did this? Yes! Nervous as hell. Would I get email complaints on the first day of school? Would parents try to move their children out of my class? Would my school administration support me? But once I was legally married, I made it a point to come out like this every single year. I stood in the firm place of righteousness. Some of my straight colleagues used a similar presentation. I almost never had students question me. Every so often, a student will say something like: "Your wife. But you can't have a wife."

When a child says something like that, I respond with something like this: "Every family is different. Some people live with their grandma, some people live with a foster parent, some kids live with one parent for part of the week and another parent for another part, and some kids have two parents they live with. This is what my family looks like. Who lives in your family? Talk with your table partner about who you live with or what your favorite food is." After they have time to talk, I say, "Now, let's look at our next math problem."

Coming out eventually became a part of my first-day routine. Honestly, I was always afraid I would get an angry email or complaint. I felt that fear and faced it, anyway. That fear lessened after a few years and, miraculously, it never occurred after we were legally married.

I felt like I had the blessing of the state, and we became legally married. What can the students' parents say? I'm sure plenty, but I have a level of confidence after our legal marriage that I didn't have before.

It was a huge deal to me to move from calling my partner, my spouse to wife, legally. Both at work and outside of work, we were simply an out couple. Everyone knew we were gay because we didn't hide it.

I loved being able to call Jay my wife. It was so different from my first years of teaching (1999) where I was terrified of what would happen if people found out I was a lesbian. There was no legal protection in the school district I worked in. My worst fear almost came true, and I had a parent figure out I was a lesbian on her own. She then told me she would attempt to get me fired and was going to complain to my principal. That was one of the most terrifying few days of my teaching career. From that point on, I have always been out to the administration where I work. But that changed when Jay came out as trans.

Once again, I was back in the earlier stages of coming out. Would I get a parent complaint if they found out? Will my current principal be supportive? Unfortunately, how someone reacts to supporting gays and lesbians is not a guide for how someone will support trans individuals.

On top of that, how does one even come out as having a trans spouse at work? At this point, I wasn't thinking about coming out to students, but to my colleagues who had known Jay for years. He often came with the kids when they were younger and ate lunch with me. They all knew I had a wife, and the majority were accepting. But would they be receptive of a trans spouse now?

Jay and I talked to various trans people to see how they handled this. One thing we heard was the idea of coming out in a letter. When I came out as a lesbian, I told everyone slowly. The idea of coming out all at once in a letter sounded so much better. We wouldn't need to have a million conversations. We would not have to see people's initial reactions. It could happen all at once.

Some people in my spouse's therapy group also used letters or a post on social media. Some friends we knew that shared a similar situation, let us see a copy of the letter they sent when their husband came out.

It was decided. Jay would come out to the world in a letter. We drafted the letter, edited it, and rewrote some more until we were satisfied with the wording and emotional feeling. Then we each sent a version of it to the people in our lives. We wanted the letter to reflect that I felt okay with everything, which I did and do. We hoped others would feel the same way, but that would be up to them.

Here is the letter I sent.

March 2019

Dear friends,

I have some news to share about our family. After a lot of time and thought, my spouse has come to realize that he is transgender (FTM or Female to Male). Coming to understand and accept this has been a long journey, really decades in the making. It culminated this past fall and winter when my spouse could finally say it out loud for the first time. It feels important and right for my spouse to transition to a more authentic gender identity, including a new name and pronouns.

We've been slowly sharing the news. Here are some questions you might have:

How are you and the kids? What will the kids call you?

Of course, this process has involved a lot of emotions. I have been through just about every possible feeling, as has Jay! Thankfully, after 18 years together, the two of us are doing really well :) The kids have been lovely, curious, resilient, and accepting. They are still calling Jay Mama for now, but it may shift over time. (The kids now call him Jay, but at the time of writing the letter, that had not happened.) *We know that these language shifts may feel awkward, and they do to us too, but over time, we are confident that everyone will adjust.*

What about this new name and pronoun thing? What if I make a mistake?

Chapter 5

My spouse has a new name: Jay

We used letters from the original first and middle names to come up with it. We are also going to be using he/him pronouns. It's going to be a long process, so if you make a mistake, don't worry! Just do your best and over time it will feel more natural. I/we are grateful for your efforts :)

Why is this change necessary? What is gender transition even about?

After a lifetime of doing every possible thing to deny this part of himself, he is ready to live as his complete self. Jay has felt a sense of difference his entire life, going back to around second grade. When he came out as gay at age 21, it seemed like that must explain everything. Jay knew trans people who had to give up everything (career, family, friends) in order to transition, and wasn't sure he could go through with that, so he stuffed it down instead. Now, at age 40, he can finally, joyfully, accept his whole self.

Now what?

We are including you in this news because you are part of our community, and we love you. Thank you for your support in this. We are excited about this new phase of our lives.

With much love,

With the letter written, we just needed to decide when to deliver the news.

Neither of us really liked the idea of sending the letter and then walking into work/school the next day. What if some people had read the letter and other people hadn't? What if people needed time to process? Would a weekend be enough time?

Thankfully, Spring Break was coming up. Jay, the children, and I were all going to Phoenix, Arizona for a family get-together. We would send the letter on Friday, after school.

Within the course of a few minutes, we emailed the letter to our work colleagues, including my principal. We also emailed the letter out to the parents in all three of the children's classrooms and their teachers. We wanted everyone to find out at the same time.

We pressed send, crossed our fingers, and tried to think about anything else. We decided to not post to our social media accounts until later. And we put away our phones.

We were apprehensive. People were okay with us being a lesbian couple, but how would they feel about Jay transitioning? How were people going to respond? How many people would give us no response? Would people be loving and accepting? Would we lose friends over this? Would our children lose friends over us? What would it be like to walk to school on Monday after Spring Break? We were a bundle of emotions.

Within minutes, we started hearing buzzes on our phones. Emails started rolling in. We were both overwhelmed by the celebration, support, and welcoming we received from our community. Many people wrote to share their congratulations and unconditional love for us. The initial responses were all quite positive, and time would tell what would happen with everyone else.

We then boarded a plane the very next day to go on vacation. Touching down in Phoenix, I wondered what would it be like to see Jay's brother and sister and his cousins? How would the extended family react? There were many people I hadn't met before that would be at the family reunion/Spring Vacation. What kind of reception would we receive?

I am an introverted person at the best of times. Some people compare being extroverted as like a solar-powered battery. The more they are around other people, the more energy they receive. Introverted people are like rechargeable batteries. Time with people wears me out and I need time alone (writing, napping, reading) to recharge.

If normally I am an A battery, this trip I felt more like an AAA battery. I had less to give and needed more time to myself. Coming out to people was draining. Change felt draining. Being around extended family members was even more draining.

Thankfully, though, we did lots of low-key activities during the trip. I recharged by writing and journaling. We all swam in a pool every day, went to the botanical gardens, and had a lovely vacation. Throughout the week, more and more emails came into both of our inboxes, mostly positive, supportive notes. We received so much love from our extended community members. Of course, some people didn't respond at all. That spoke volumes. Or did it? It was hard to know.

We kept wondering, are they not responding because they are on vacation? Or because they don't think it's a big deal? Or perhaps they are not supportive. (All three would turn out to be true in various cases.)

There were some individuals who wrote things that were less than supportive. Their messages were really hard to read, especially when some of those individuals were family members. When I would read those letters, it felt like a punch to the gut. My chest felt tight with physical pain. Tension built up in my head and behind my eyes. I think we chose to mostly not respond to those emails. If this happens to you, it is really your decision if you respond. You do not owe anyone a reply.

A few times, I would share these less than positive comments with friends. I mostly heard things like, "Well, what did you expect? You know they are religious. Of course, they responded that way." Or "Most people aren't like that."

I didn't want to hear excuses or explanations about why some people were responding negatively. We knew not everyone would be supportive. All I wanted to hear was, "I'm so sorry. That must feel hard." Or better yet, "How does that make you feel?" Thankfully, those less than supportive people that emailed us were not the same ones vacationing with us!

I continued journaling. Especially after reading some emails that questioned Jay and his identity. Some people could not wrap their heads around the idea that just because Jay had been masking who he was (he passed as a woman), he did not feel comfortable and hadn't been true to himself.

Jay studied how females interacted and was very perceptive. He could follow the social rules so well that people around him suspected nothing was up. But he was not his authentic self. A few people couldn't understand that just because he passed well as a female didn't mean

Chapter 5

that he felt like one. Just because he could act a certain way, didn't mean that was who he was. I'm not extroverted, no matter how outgoing I might act in a certain place and time. Jay is not a female, no matter how well he can act in that role at any time.

Here is one of the entries I wrote after reading one of our less than supportive emails. This is slightly edited for clarity. It was helpful to write. I responded back and forth with this person eventually, but this writing was just for me.

3/25

What do I wish other people knew right now?

This change is hard. It is hard for Jay. Most people do not wake up after 40 years to realize they have spent 40 years living as a girl, only to realize that this was not who they are.

Jay needs to be vulnerable. How can he express how difficult this is without having people doubt his truth? Is it possible for him to share with others that this has been a hard process, terrifying, and yet is still what is true and honest?

How do I know that this is honest and, at his core, the truth? I know when I am experiencing deep peace, and another person is expressing their core. I can feel that when Jay is calm, centered, and not feeling anxious, he always comes back to the same thing. He is trans. He is Jay. He is joy.

I want him to have the space to share his full range of feelings without fear of being judged as unworthy. Isn't that what we all want? To really be heard and to really be seen for who we are?

And at its core, we all are one. We are all pieces of the divine having this human experience. Apparently, the divine in Jay needed to have this fuller experience of moving through this world as being perceived as both female and then non-binary and, in the future, as male. I don't know why.

Apparently, my spirit needed to experience what I'm going through. It might not be fun at times. Other times, I can see the genuine gift I am being given.

My life is not mine to control. It is a journey that I have the honor of experiencing. I can either resist and cause friction and pain in my life, or I can embrace it. I still feel pain, but I also feel immense joy, peace, love, and everything else there is to feel when I embrace life.

His outside appearance might change, but who Jay is at his core has always been there. He is the person we have all always loved and will continue to love. Simply, he is starting the process of making his outsides match, best as possible, to how he feels on the inside.

And he needs laughter and joy and fun. This doesn't have to be so serious all the time. There is silliness, and awkwardness, and everything else. We can have fun with it. That's ok!

We went to a pool yesterday and Jay was in his swim trunks with a rash guard. Seeing Jay play in the pool with the kids was so beautiful. Last night, he said it was one of the first times in the pool where he felt fully present playing with the kids. He wasn't self-conscious about how he looked or where he was. He was there in the pool, having fun with the kids, enjoying life.

I want more laughter, lightness, and joy for all of us. And I finally understand that the only way to have that lightness, joy, and peace is to accept all our feelings. The happier and sadder

Chapter 5

ones. We can mute all our feelings, or we can embrace them, but we can't have it both ways.

Being around so many people, many of whom I didn't know well, was stressful for me. I continued journaling and writing most days. I also did a lot of tapping that vacation (thank you therapist!). Tapping and saying honest things was a release valve. It helped me get back to a calmer place.

Once or twice a day, I would take some time completely by myself in the hotel room. I would sit on the bed, or in the bathroom, and do my tapping. I would say all the thoughts I was having out loud while tapping the points above my eye, to the side of my eye, under my eye, under my nose, and on my chest. I really worked to not censor myself, no matter what I was thinking. I put on the timer for 10 minutes and then let the words flow out.

This stream of consciousness sounded something like this:

- "I'm sick and tired of being around people.
- I just want quiet. I don't want to talk to anyone.
- I'm sick of small talk. Fuck the small talk.
- Someone, ask me something real. Like actually ask me how I feel and listen to me. Hello? How do you think I feel about my spouse transitioning? I'm glad for all the support, I am, but talk to me.
- Do I have to be the supportive spouse at all

times? Don't you think I have some emotions about this? This sucks. Everything sucks."

I would talk for ten whole minutes out loud. Normally, by minute seven or eight, I was feeling much calmer. By minute ten, I sometimes even ran out of things to say, even after repeating my sentences quite a few times. By the end, I felt better most of the time.

I think I felt torn between being supportive of Jay and having my own real full emotions. My full range of emotions was messy. I didn't feel one way all the time. Sometimes I felt fine, other times I was still in shock about the whole situation, other times I was excited. Every so often, I would wake up and forget that my life had changed. Then I would remember and wonder, how the hell did this happen?

After taking those periodic ten minutes in our hotel room, I would come out ready to have fun and enjoy the family. Sometimes I felt like I was masking my own emotions. I hadn't quite figured out how to be authentically me and supportive all at the same time.

That being said, we had many wonderful adventures together during that vacation. We all horsed around in the pool, splashing one another. We visited an aquarium, and the kids were able to do a modified version of scuba diving. Joan was too young, so she watched the big kids while hanging out with Grandma. Joan had her birthday and turned nine years old.

We went to the botanical gardens. It is one of my favorite places to visit and a highlight of our trips. That

Chapter 5

year, the gardens even had a butterfly exhibit. The whole extended family headed out together for the butterfly garden on one of our last days together. I arrived at the garden feeling like my AAA batteries had been fully discharged and needed some me time badly. So, even though I was with our extended family and children, I went off on my own for a bit. Everyone was in the garden exhibit, but I slowed down. I felt compelled to sit on the ground and look at a butterfly that had landed on a flower.

A few minutes later, that same butterfly flapped its wings, took off from the flower, and landed on my dress, right on my chest.

I held my breath for a moment and then breathed deeply. I felt a calmness spread throughout my body. This felt like a sacred moment.

The butterfly sat for a while and then started doing what looked like a little dance. It wiggled and moved its thorax and then touched my chest. I could clearly see the top of the butterfly, but not what it was doing.

After five minutes of this, one of the exhibit helpers came by and pointed out that the butterfly was actually laying eggs on me.

I felt chills. Wow!

The butterfly minders carefully lifted the butterfly and moved it so the butterfly could lay its eggs in a better location. Looking at the butterfly laying eggs that would become a caterpillar, I heard a voice in my head. *This is Jay. The caterpillar turns into a butterfly. He might look different on the outside. But that was the plan. It is all part of his metamorphosis into this beautiful being he was meant to be.*

I eventually stood up, feeling quite recharged and alive. I rejoined the family and continued to look through the gardens and walk around the botanical exhibits. That evening, I took another bit of time to myself. I strolled in town to look in some of the art galleries. Scottsdale is known for its art galleries.

Normally, we just look at the artwork for fun. But walking around, I saw something that made my heart skip a beat. This piece of art had a blue butterfly and a green butterfly etched into a red iridescent piece of metal. The art piece spoke to me.

I suddenly had a thought. Jay's favorite color is blue, and my favorite color is green.

I had to show this piece of art to Jay. That afternoon, Jay and I went to look at the artwork. His parents watched the kids so we could have a few minutes to ourselves. I explained how the butterfly represented Jay becoming his true self and how this piece of art spoke to me. We agreed that the artwork was beautiful and bought it. We now have this metal etching of the two butterflies in our bedroom. Whenever I look at the butterfly, I feel happy and joyful and remember that moment in the garden.

Soon after buying the butterfly etching, it was time to end our family vacation. Jay and the kids traveled back to home, while I traveled on to Mexico to visit my parents. I hadn't seen them since Jay had come out via the letter to them. We had only talked on the phone.

Jay, the kids, and I drove to the Phoenix airport

Chapter 5

together. Then I gave everyone hugs and kisses and headed for the international terminal.

Finding a snack at the terminal, I sat down to read a book I had been waiting to read. Eventually, I boarded the flight and flew to Guadalajara. My parents met me at the airport, and we had a packed weekend. We celebrated my mother's birthday with a large party, met friends, went out to eat at their favorite restaurants, and hung out. I spent time with my uncle and his girlfriend, who also came down to celebrate my mom's birthday. My parents had done the job of coming out for us to my uncle and aunt and all of their friends, which was really appreciated. Everyone had lots of questions to ask.

On our second night, we went out to dinner with some of my parents' friends and my uncle and his girlfriend. Sitting outside on a patio surrounded by potted plants, while drinking a margarita and eating Nopales Rellenos, I listened to their questions. When did I find out? How long did he know before he told you? Does he look different now? How did you tell the children? How did the children respond?

I know many spouses and trans individuals don't like questions and find them invasive. That is understandable. Most of the time, I don't mind. As long as a person is polite and kind, I'll happily answer most questions. Most questions are what I call curiosity questions. Curiosity questions are about learning more, not necessarily about connecting. That evening in the restaurant I mainly got these types of questions from my parent's friends and family.

Sitting on the patio, while the sun set and the temperature cooled, we talked until closing time. Through the evening, I felt my uncle and his girlfriend move from curiosity to understanding the transition more. I appreciated they were talking to me about what was going on in my life.

And I was honestly happy that Jay and the children had not come to Mexico. I was able to act as a buffer and handle the questions without worrying about words hurting him or causing him discomfort with my family.

The next day, we met up with more family friends. I received more questions, but these were different. They wanted to know how *I* was really doing. Not in a "I would leave my spouse if that happened," or "that's wild... you are so amazing" type of way, either. They had a level of compassion for my experience without feeling sorry for me or imagining that I'm the hero of some outlandish tale—which I am not!!! They talked with me, holding a more nuanced view of the experience. This was one of the first times I could have a conversation like this with a few close family friends who had been married for many years and who understood the ups and downs of any successful long-term relationship.

It helped that at least one of these couples had known Jay and me for over a decade before the transition. I felt seen and heard. I left that evening knowing my parents' closest friends supported me, and so did my family. That was and continues to be such a blessing.

Before long, it was time to return home. This would be our first time back at work and school after having sent the

Chapter 5

coming out letter to everyone. The adults were all a bundle of nerves that morning. Although the kids knew the letter had been sent, they did not seem to think this was a big deal. My heartbeat raced, and I had no appetite for breakfast at all. There was no way Jay or I could drink anything with caffeine in it, either. Nervously, I drove to work, and Jay drove the three children to school. As I walked in, a few teachers connected and talked with me. The ones who reached out were supportive and kind. Thankfully, teaching is the type of job where from the moment the first bell rings to the end of the day you are just going, going, going. There is barely time to eat lunch most days. After the initial conversations, I taught my class and then the day was over in a flash. Amazingly, it had all gone smoothly for both Jay and me. It almost seemed too good to be true. Were most people really this supportive or were we only talking to the people who were supportive? Only time would tell.

A few days later, we received a message on Jay's phone. Our youngest daughter Joan was planning a sleepover for her ninth birthday party the weekend after spring break. We planned it for this date because that was the only date her best friend, Emily, could sleep over. Joan had a few other kids she occasionally hung out with, but Emily was her person. Joan and Emily had been inseparable since preschool. They enjoyed sleepovers, playing together, and stuck together like peanut butter and jelly. The message was from Emily's mom. She said that Emily would not be able to make Joan's party after all.

Jay immediately said this was exactly what he feared

would happen if he came out. We had discussed this quite a bit before ever sending out the letter and were prepared that this might be a possibility. We just hoped it wouldn't affect the children. I offered to call Emily's mom so he would not have to be part of that conversation. I felt like if there was an opportunity for me to spare Jay having those conversations, I would do so. I acted as a social buffer when possible.

I called back to find out what had happened. Even though Emily's mom had called Jay, I didn't want him to have to talk about this with her. We had chosen the date because it worked for Emily's family. Clearly, something was up, and I had a hunch it was about Jay.

I made the call. I remember dialing the number while walking in our backyard, pacing up and down the green lawn. Jay stood nearby, watching me in the beginning until I waved him off, saying that I was fine. Emily's mom and I started with some chitchat about vacation. Then we discussed Jay coming out, and she claimed to have "so much sympathy for me and everything I must be going through." She demonstrated her "incredible sympathy" for me in the next sentence by letting me know her daughter could not sleep over at our house anymore.

The mom said, "We don't want Emily to get confused. We are afraid if she sleeps at your house, she will be."

I reminded the mom that we had planned this weekend so Emily could come and reminded her that Emily was Joan's best friend. In the end, she said she would talk to her husband. They compromised and decided maybe Emily could come for part of the party, but not sleep over.

Chapter 5

Joan was distraught. We had planned this party for a time when her best friend could sleep over. Now that would not happen. We had made her wait until she was nine to have her first sleepover. Having two older siblings, she had been anticipating this first birthday sleepover for years.

As it would turn out, that was the last time Emily came to our house. Soon after that, Emily stopped playing with Joan at school and eventually stopped even talking, making eye contact, or acknowledging that our daughter even existed. For months, Joan begged us every week to call her family for a play date. Every Saturday morning, she would ask us to call Emily. It took us a while to really understand what was happening, but one day Jay witnessed Joan call out to her friend at school during drop-off and watched Emily turn away, whisper to a friend, and blatantly ignore Joan. It was clear that Emily would no longer be in Joan's life.

The school would not acknowledge that this had anything to do with Jay coming out. The school kept on saying, "This just happens in second and third grade. Kids' friendships change." But it was crystal clear to us that the coming-out letter was the beginning of the end of that friendship. It was frustrating that every time we brought up the connection, there was a total denial that there could ever be a relationship between Jay coming out and the friendship ending. This was devastating to witness. I think it was especially hard on Jay. It was one of his worst fears that coming out as trans would hurt his family. There was nothing we could do to protect Joan from this pain. And the pain went on for months and months.

In the end, Joan would make new friends, but that process would take over a year. If your child is in this situation, I've included a few books in the reference section on making friends that might be helpful.

Now, many years later, Joan sometimes still brings up how hard this time was. Her new friends are more solid, accepting, and loving than before. But it was an awful process to witness the pain and suffering our nine-year-old child had to experience because of transphobia.

It continues to baffle me to this day that the family was okay with us as a lesbian couple, but not as a straight appearing couple. Transphobia is a strange beast, and we have learned repeatedly that people can be okay with gays and lesbians but not trans individuals.

Around this time, Bubbles started to sleep in Joan's room every night. She needed the extra comfort and Bubbles, now affectionately called our "therapy dog", was ready to give a cuddle any time. Joan needed some extra love. Bubbles continued to be an incredible gift and one that just kept on giving to us. Some days, I felt like Jay's grandma brought Bubbles into our life and was there to watch over us during this time of transition.

Amazingly, neither Liz nor Cole lost any friends over Jay coming out. Only Joan had this experience. The parents of Liz's and Cole's friends continued to accept them unconditionally. Now when we have a child sleep over for the first time, Jay or I make a point to be sure the family is aware that we are a queer family. There is no chance of

Chapter 5

repeating the Emily situation, and we figure it is better to find out early in a friendship if a family is not okay with us.

So, we had survived the first two rounds of coming out. Everyone in our immediate and extended family knew about Jay and his transition. Everyone I worked with knew, everyone at the kids' school knew. It was nice to not be hiding and just have it be out. That was a relief, no matter the consequences.

While there were some less than supportive individuals in these places, most people ranged from tolerant to accepting to embracing. This outcome was way better than we had feared and a tremendous relief.

Now, we could focus on the next hurdle—Jay's first T shot.

Chapter 6

April

Navigating this next month of our lives felt like programming a new destination on a GPS, uncertain whether we were heading towards an entirely new place or merely taking a different route to the same loving relationship. Amidst the tsunami of emotions surrounding Jay's approaching first shot day, my fears of a new set of directions were palpable. Jay had changed his name, his pronouns, his wardrobe and was living his life openly. So far, though, he had not taken any medical steps. Testosterone would change that. It's important to know that not everyone takes medical steps for transition, but for Jay, it was important to him, and so it was important for me as well.

In moments of calm, I realized that, despite the anxiety, we were still on the same path—our bond, our love, remained unwavering. It was akin to noticing that, despite the unfamiliar roads and detours, the GPS ultimately guided us to a familiar place. In my calmest moments, I was able to notice and appreciate the new scenery I never would have observed on the old path.

While the journey might have been different, the destination, our loving relationship, remained constant. The landscape might have shifted, but the core of our connection endured, guiding us through uncharted emotional territories while reassuring me that, despite the uncertainties, our destination remained unchanged.

The last few months had been a lot to handle. I had gone from not knowing anything in November about Jay's deep discomfort with presenting as a woman to having a testosterone shot day coming up in April. I think some days I was still in shock, but other days not so much.

Navigating the lead-up to Jay's first shot day felt like being inside a bustling pinball machine, where my thoughts acted as levers, propelling my emotions in unpredictable loops. Despite being genuinely excited for Jay about 90% of the time, that remaining 10% brought about extreme emotions, particularly centered on fears concerning testosterone and its potential impact on his sexuality and personality.

I was still terrified that testosterone would turn him into a gay man. I didn't come up with this wild idea in my head. Reading online, it sounded like some people have their orientation clarified after starting hormones.

I brought this fear to the spouses' group to hear what they had to say. Most people in the group had spouses that were transitioning from male to female. It sounded like, among the committed long-term couples, a transition from

Chapter 6

female to male with a sexuality change as well was less common to occur. Still, there were some individuals who had experienced their spouse's sexual orientation shift as they started hormone replacement therapy.

From what I heard, it sounded like when a person realized they were more flexible than they realized, it was because they had been suppressing this emotion all along. The testosterone only makes the attraction clearer. At least this seemed to be the message I heard. So, unless Jay had some underlying tendencies in that direction, I didn't need to be afraid. And he didn't. Of course, I had no idea that Jay had felt like a guy, either. That probably explained why I had some worries that maybe there was more to the story. There was only one way to find out. We had to see what happened after Jay started taking T. I had to trust him when he said he was still attracted to me.

But what about my attraction to him?

Assuming Jay's sexuality was not about to change, mine was a different story. I would move from being with a woman to being with a man. To be honest, I felt afraid I wouldn't be attracted to Jay anymore. I had come out as a lesbian years ago. While I definitely tended to be attracted to more androgynous, butcher women, I felt a strong connection with only women. I loved being a lesbian and having a wife. I felt happy and settled with everything prior to the transition.

A few times, I tried to imagine if I could be attracted to a guy. In addition to that day at the bowling alley with the man beside our lane, I also let my mind travel down this path in early January. We got together with someone who was trans who had a similar build to Jay. We were sitting at their kitchen table, and I remember looking at Jay and looking at our friend and trying to imagine Jay having the same beard. How would he look? Could I find a beard on him attractive? I really wasn't sure. I think I was so consumed with anxiety that I talked little during our meal and wasn't the best guest. All I could do was imagine what Jay would look like after transitioning.

My other major fear around testosterone was that it would affect Jay's emotions. I worried it would make him angry or shut down his ability to express himself, or even have emotions anymore. Again, I had read online that some people said that after their spouse went on testosterone, they no longer seemed to have access to their full range of emotions. Would Jay skyrocket to anger easily? Or would he turn into a quiet guy who was not comfortable expressing his feelings and thoughts? While the internet can be helpful, to connect with other people going through similar experiences, there are a lot of scary clickbait type stories to wade through. I personally have a hard time expressing anger or being around angered people. When another person raises their voice, I immediately get a strong fight-or-flight response. I pick up on cues early when someone is getting irritated, often before other people are aware that something is happening. It is something I'm extra sensitive to. That Jay might become easily angered sounded worrisome to me.

The last major concern I had prior to testosterone was how it would affect his sex drive. For many people, the testosterone shots caused a dramatic increase in libido. I honestly wasn't sure how I felt about that type of change. I was happily married to a 40-year-old and didn't want to suddenly have someone with a teenage drive as my spouse. While generally I have a stronger drive than Jay, I wasn't sure how that would be if the tables were turned. Maybe that would be good?

In all I read, I wasn't sure what to believe. The websites threw out every outcome, but they could have been over-hyped ideas that were fishing for clicks. I didn't know what to trust or who to trust. I figured that perhaps most people who were happy and doing fine were not writing online about their experiences. Maybe what I was seeing online was a skewed sample. We would need to find out on our own how testosterone affected Jay.

Sometimes, the fear and anxiety felt like being stuck in that pinball game again, where my thoughts controlled the chaos. The ball kept bouncing back to the same place. It was overwhelming. My mind couldn't shake off the worry about how testosterone might change things for us. My heart would race, and my stomach twisted into knots. I tried hard to distract myself, focus on anything else, but it felt impossible. My body just wouldn't cooperate; the discomfort was too much.

When I would get to constant discomfort, I relied on my tools. I also had a few months of practice that proved to me the feelings would subside. I could tap, I could write my feelings, play piano, distract myself with something, or just let the feelings be and wash over me.

I was beginning to feel more trusting in the process of navigating my own emotions. I found new ways to calm down my mind, to dial down the frenzy of anxious thoughts, making it less like a crazy pinball game. It started with a simple belief: things would change slowly, giving me the chance to adapt. This was one of the most helpful thoughts I had that could calm down my mind. I repeated it over and over to myself.

I thought about our kids growing up. They had transformed from tiny tots to pre-teens, right in front of us. It was so gradual, not a sudden shift, yet every day brought something new. And despite their changing appearances, my love for them remained constant. It made me realize that maybe Jay's journey would be similar, a gradual evolution where each step felt more natural and less jarring.

With the children, we were both able to appreciate and enjoy all the changes and react with excitement. What if I could have the same approach to Jay changing? I hoped I could celebrate Jay's changes along the way, if only I wasn't consumed by my fears and anxieties.

One particular day in April, I honestly felt extremely guilty about my fears. I knew that if the situation were reversed, Jay would be supportive of me. And I wanted nothing more than to be supportive of Jay. Even now, I wish the fears and anxieties never existed. I wish that I could have sailed through the whole transition, by being accepting, loving and celebratory all the time. I have some guilt about not seeing right from the beginning that Jay was always who he was. He had just been superb at passing. Still, my fears were real and rational. I just needed to find ways to face them.

Chapter 6

Often, when I was having a hard time, I found that changing my location and getting some exercise helped. Going out on a walk might be the last thing I felt like doing when I was anxious, but it made an enormous difference.

One day, I decided I needed to get out of my mind and move my body. Tapping hadn't worked. I still felt anxious after trying to refocus on playing the piano. So I went for a walk.

A block from our house is an undeveloped piece of land where our dogs like to play and run. I took Bubbles and Tango out to sniff the grass there and ran into an older neighbor named Dalia with her terrier dog.

Dalia lives a few blocks away from me in the neighborhood and typically walks her little dog multiple times a week. She is probably in her 70s. She has short curly white hair and has always been friendly to me.

On this day, our dogs both finished their business around the same time, and we ended up walking around the neighborhood together. I was overwhelmed with emotion and ended up over sharing (maybe) about how I was having a hard time with the transition at that specific moment.

Inside my mind, I was thinking about how my old dreams of the future were disappearing. We would never be a pair of grandmas sitting on our front porch in rocking chairs while our grandchildren played in the yard. We would never be a lesbian couple at a pride parade in 2050. We would never be many things that I had envisioned in my head.

I had to release my old thoughts and dreams, but

replace them with what? I just didn't have any images in my mind of what Jay would be as a grandpa. What would we look like in three years, much less in 10 years as a couple?

I told Dalia how sad I was feeling about Jay's transition. "It is so hard. All these dreams I had for the future will not happen now. I'm happy for him, but I feel sad about all the things I thought were going to happen that aren't."

Dalia could relate to my statement. She said, "Yes. That is really hard. You know my husband Marcus passed about 6 years ago now. I still think about him every day."

I knew about her loss, and I asked her if living gets any easier. "Yes and no," she responded. "I still have moments where I miss him. I'll always love him, but I will never get to talk with him again in this life. I'll never get to see his smile again. He is really gone. But it is not all bad. It does get easier with time."

One thing she said really hit me. As Dahlia talked about how she would never get to see Marcus again, I realized just how lucky I was. I got to see Jay every day. Not only that, but I also got to experience this transition alongside him. At that moment, things shifted in my mind.

I told Dalia, "I didn't really think about it like that. Even though Jay is changing, we get to go through this together. That is good to remember."

I appreciated Dalia, and I realized what I was grieving for wasn't so much a person, but an imaginary future I had in my brain that might have never actually come to pass. Sitting on the porch in our swing when we were grandmas

Chapter 6

was just a fantasy that I created in my brain. These images were literally composed of neurons firing in a pattern that created an emotional reaction in my body. The events never actually happened. We had never sat as grandmas on a porch swinging in our rocking chairs. It was just a potential future of my imagination.

All our actual past experiences were still there. Our meeting each other and everything that we had done together still existed in my memory. It was the images of our future that needed changing, and that was what I needed to focus on.

I had once enjoyed making up the original images of what our future might look like. I had enjoyed spinning them together with Jay, but now we could do it all over again. Yes, the visualizations of potential futures would be different, but they could be just as wonderful.

I still see Dalia when I walk every so often. Sometimes I wave hello and stop to chat about our dogs, or about her granddaughter, for a few minutes. That was probably the only time in three years we mentioned Jay's transition. But that conversation had a lasting effect on me. I am eternally grateful for the perspective she gave me.

When I felt sad or grieved, which thankfully happened less and less over time, I remembered Jay was still here and with me. The future was wide open for us to create our future experiences together, better ones, where we both would get to express ourselves fully.

Jay, the essence of his person, still existed and always has existed. He always resided deep down in the girl and woman he had appeared to be for so many years. I fell in love with that essence, whether or not I knew it, because that is who Jay has always been.

I would not let my fears stop Jay from living and being his true self. He would never ask that of me, and I would not ask that of him. Part of what I have appreciated about our relationship is how much we both support each other in going after our dreams and being our best selves. Testosterone was going to be part of how Jay would become his best self.

Quickly for me, but slowly for Jay, April 16th arrived. This was the day Jay would get his first shot. I had taken the day off from school so I could be there with him. By that day, most of my fears were faced and overall, I was excited for Jay. Yes, this was a big change. Yes, I did not know how it would all work, but I wanted to be there to witness this day with him and support him fully.

That morning, I woke up not sure if I could eat breakfast. I put on my feel-good outfit that I wore on Valentine's Day. Jay wore a blue and black checkered flannel and some jeans.

After getting dressed, I woke up the kids and enjoyed some major cuddles with Bubbles while Jay started on breakfast.

Jay had planned on making all three kids a special breakfast of homemade chocolate chip waffles. Unfortunately, we had no eggs, so I went to the store for the missing ingredients. I think they knew this was Jay's first shot day, but it did not seem like such a big deal to them. They would go to school and the day would be normal for them.

Chapter 6

As I drove up the hill on my way to the grocery store, I tried to enjoy the new leaves of spring. Tulips were budding, and the daffodils were blooming. My favorite rhododendrons were almost ready to burst with color. New life was everywhere. I was a bit too anxious to really enjoy it all.

I took a quick video after I parked the car and before going into the store. This is a transcript of the recording. I've edited it somewhat for length.

Today is the morning of my spouse's first testosterone shot. I want to take a video to record my memories at this moment. I woke up feeling anxious in my stomach. Like, what is going to happen today? What is it going to be like? I know that there won't be any physical change immediately following the moment of that first shot. But it's a huge journey. It's not one that I expected to come along after 18 years of being together, but this is how I was feeling this morning.

I needed to buy some eggs at the store. As I was driving here, I took a moment to put my hand on my heart and asked spirit, higher power, please take away my fear. Please help me be present at this moment that is right now.

When I got out of the car, I released my fears. I don't know how, but I let them go. After some time, a new thought came to me. I get to learn how to give my spouse a shot.

It's shot day!

. . .

After recording the video, I felt a sense of peace come over me. I would be ok. I just needed to slow down and take this one moment at a time. I didn't need to listen to all my anxious thoughts about the future. Those thoughts did not actually know what our experience was going to be like. I could take in the day, moment by moment.

Driving home, I made it a point to notice the flowers and admire the buds. All this new growth and change were just a part of life.

I drove into the garage and gave Jay the eggs for breakfast. He quickly cracked two eggs into a bowl, poured in the milk, and measured the rest of the ingredients. In no time, he whisked up the waffle batter. After breakfast, we both took the kids to school in our minivan. Immediately after dropping them off, we drove to the other side of the city. Jay needed to go to the pharmacy to get his needles, hormones, and supplies before his appointment at the gender clinic.

Driving from the suburbs through downtown during morning rush hour can be unpredictable. We made it to the parking garage forty minutes before the appointment. We still had to get parked, get a new prescription filled, and go up to the third floor where the gender clinic was located. This would be my first time at their clinic with Jay.

We walked into the pharmacy, and Jay pushed the button to get his ticket. A white thin paper with the number A050 streamed out of the machine. Jay ripped off the ticket, and we took a picture of both of us with it. We wore huge grins on our faces, enjoying the selfie moment. We sat in the pharmacy's rows of chairs, everyone elbow to

Chapter 6

elbow. In a few minutes, A050 was called up to the counter. Jay was nervous about how this part would go, but the tech approached this prescription like any other. Jay got his first testosterone bottle, needles, alcohol wipes, and everything else he needed. We bounded out of the pharmacy and up the stairs. It was time to go up to the gender clinic.

Sitting outside the clinic, we were the only people around. I asked Jay how he was feeling. He had this huge grin on his face, emanating happiness. Even thinking about it now, I feel a lightness in my chest and a big smile on my face. We were whispering in the hallway, even though no one was there. The gender clinic did not even have its own waiting room. We literally waited in a hallway. It felt a bit strange to be so out in the open. I asked him why we were whispering when no one was around, and we both laughed a little.

I asked Jay what was in the bag with the prescriptions. He showed me the different needles. He looked at the needles and said, "I'm happy to know they are smaller than I thought."

Jay lifted one needle, still in the packet, and showed it to me. The needle looked both big and small, all at the same time. The idea of injecting something every week sounded so brave.

Looking in the bag, I commented, "I can't believe how many needles you have. That is crazy. They gave you a lot."

Jay explained each shot needed two needles. A larger one to draw up the testosterone from the vial and another for injecting. He held up the needle used to draw up the testosterone. "I thought the needles were going to be this big. But look at these tiny little guys. So *tiny*. These will be fine."

I was happy that Jay felt confident.

"Jay?"

A nursing assistant had entered the empty hallway and interrupted our still-whispered conversations. She took us back to the clinic, where we waited for the provider to come. Before long, it was time for Jay to learn how to give himself a shot.

He started by washing his hands and then he sat down with the bottle of testosterone, sterile alcohol wipe pads, needles, and sharps container all out on a silver medical tray. The moment had come.

"So, do I give the shot in my stomach?" Jay asked.

"You just need to rotate sides on your thighs," the nurse explained. "Your shot day is Tuesday, so you need to rotate from the right to the left side of your body, going back and forth each week." She then took out the white prescription box that held the testosterone. The box was maybe two inches tall by four inches wide and were two little boxes connected to each other. She opened the box from the bottom, took out a small vial of testosterone with a red cap on it, and placed it on the tray.

His doctor planned on having him start with a lower dose of testosterone for the first three months. This is common and gives a body time to adjust. It would also give me some time to adjust to slower changes. I appreciated Jay and his doctor for doing it that way. She pointed

Chapter 6

out that even though the vial said it was a single dose, Jay would use each one for up to four weeks.

"Make sure you finish one vial before you start the next one," she instructed.

I sat to the side, watching the entire experience. I was so glad I had taken the day off from work to be there with Jay. What a special day. I wouldn't have wanted him to do this on his own. I knew he was excited, of course, but it was so important to me that we go together. This medicine would make a huge difference in both of our lives, and I wanted to be there to participate from the beginning. I felt proud of Jay for getting to this point and genuinely interested in the process.

Many years ago, I had to give myself a shot in the thigh. I was so nervous. I had a terrible migraine and needed to give myself an injection to help control the pain. At the time of the shot, I couldn't remember how to do it and I was terrified that I would somehow hurt myself if I didn't give it correctly. I can remember sitting down and taking a bunch of deep breaths, saying to myself, "You can do this. You can do this." And then plunging the needle in and pressing down the syringe.

I was so glad Jay was learning exactly what he needed to do. I was relieved that the nurse was going over all the steps so clearly. That way, if he got nervous, it would all be clear. I was also watching and recording everything for him, so he could always go back and rewatch the video if he had questions. I don't think he ever needed to do that, though.

The nurse explained all the supplies in order. "Here is

the vial, the needle to pull up the medicine, the needle to inject, the syringe, two alcohol wipes and a bandaid."

Jay popped the top of the red bottle of vial. He put on the needle for pulling up the testosterone and correctly got the syringe ready to draw up the T. He was explained the three major steps: how to prepare and draw up the syringe, how to inject the syringe, and how to properly dispose of the needles.

Then he held the needle, took a breath, and plunged it into the right side of his body. I stood by, watching him. He pushed the medicine in. "Oh," he said. "That stings a little bit."

"It's just the medicine going in," the nurse told him. "That's totally normal."

And two seconds later, it was done. Jay had a huge grin on his face. "I did it. That was so easy," he said with some shock and a lot of delight in his voice.

Watching the whole thing, I felt so proud of him. He gave himself a shot. That takes serious bravery. And there he was, the same person I had loved for over 18 years, just looking like he did the moment before.

We walked back to our minivan and decided to go out for a celebratory brunch. I asked Jay how he felt after his first shot. Laughing, he said, "Well, my voice feels a little hoarse. Maybe it is changing already." We giggled together as he drove out of the parking lot.

Jay and I finished the celebration by buying some fried chicken at a restaurant with some homemade lemonade. It was a beautiful sunny April day. I didn't know how the

Chapter 6

changes were going to affect us as a family, but we were in it together and it was clear that this was what Jay needed.

Chapter 7

May

Every Tuesday, Jay gave himself his shot. Some of these days, one of the kids would join him in the bathroom to watch. Liz found the process of testosterone being pulled up into a syringe fascinating. She even helped a few times in the beginning. This weekly procedure became a family affair we all looked forward to for the first month. It was exciting and new for us all. We wanted to be a part of it, and we were also happy for Jay to get this part of his life started.

Even though I had some fears about the whole thing, the anticipation of the changes to come outweighed the fears. In particular, I was expecting the change in his voice.

Each week, Jay would record a video of his voice to capture the slight changes.

- "This is my voice two weeks on T."
- "This is my voice three weeks on T."

- "This is my voice, one month on T."

I think we both thought that his voice was going to change rapidly. We were wrong.

From week to week, we would listen to the first recording and the new recording. There wasn't much of a distinguishable change. I found the rate of change reassuring, though at the same time, I knew it felt painfully slow to Jay. He had waited with so much expectancy for each shot day and now had to wait longer for the medicine to affect his body. The gradual change, however, gave us more time to spread the word.

While Jay followed the weekly shot schedule and waited for the expected outcome, we decided it was a good time to inform the neighbors. Thankfully, we already had the letter that we had shared with the school community and my work.

I knew that coming out was really stressful for Jay. I knew he would get a vulnerability hangover. So, it made sense to have me be the one to come out to the neighbors. Having me share the news would hopefully set the tone that I was okay with the transition and supportive of my spouse. It would also protect Jay from any potentially negative reactions.

Neither of us was sure how our neighbors would take the news. We live on the edge between a city and the suburbs. While most people might think that our city is a purely liberal part of the country, we regularly see Fox News played on many of the TVs through windows. We

Chapter 7

live in a very purple neighborhood that possibly tilts conservative. Reactions could go either way.

I felt torn. It was not like I wanted to go around and explain everything to our neighbors, but I really didn't want this information to spread via gossip. And it would soon become obvious. Eventually, Jay would start growing a beard. His voice would deepen. The neighbors would hear me calling him by a different name and pronoun. It seemed like coming out would prevent a lot of confusion.

So, I braved the neighbors. I had our coming-out letter in my hands and walked out the front door and up the hill to our first neighbor. I walked past the no-solicitors sign and rang the webcam doorbell. I could hear a dog barking, but no one came to the door for a few moments. Then Ella opened the door.

"Hi Ella. How are you doing?" I said, thinking how no one ever explains how to have this type of conversation.

What does one say to a neighbor? *"Hi. I know you think we are a lesbian couple, which I'm sure was neighborhood news when we moved in, but actually, my spouse is transgender."* No, that is obviously not how I was going to start the conversation.

So here I was, standing in front of our neighbor with a letter. After some chit-chat, I said, "I wanted to share some news about our family with you," while handing her the letter.

Ella took the letter and read it right there, with me standing on the doorstep. "Oh, wow. My daughter has a friend that is transitioning in her class. How are the kids taking it? Are they okay?" I was immediately relieved because I had no clue how Ella was going to take the news. This seemed like a positive reaction.

After going over how the kids were fine, I said goodbye and walked to the next neighbor. So far, one neighbor down and five more neighbors to go on our little side street.

Overall, the neighbors were all polite to me, even the ones that have Fox News playing regularly through their windows. One of the most conservative neighbors invited me into her living room and wanted to chat for a while. She was welcoming and mostly wanted to know how the children were handling everything. That was the most common question I received. The neighbor we were closest to had questions about how I was doing as well. She wanted to know if I was okay with everything and if it had been hard. She asked if Jay had known this for a long time. The questions were coming from a place of kind curiosity, and I was happy to talk with her.

I don't know how all the neighbors really thought about the whole situation, only what they said to me and in our "liberal city" they all know to say the right thing to our faces. I know that one of the five continues to this day to post transphobic things online. I'm glad it was me and not Jay who explained the situation to her. It is weird to think that her family can be kind and polite to our faces and even invite me into her house while posting negative things on social media. Thankfully, we don't have to interact with them online and we thankfully only see them every so often in real life.

After coming out to the neighbors, we had a home

Chapter 7

project we needed to work on. We'd purchased a magnetic screen door, mainly because our three cats had a habit of bolting out the back door whenever they get a chance and we wanted to prevent them from running outside. Plus, we wanted to keep the bugs out. You know, fresh air is great, but waking up to mosquito bites? No thanks.

After talking about it on and off for a long time, I finally ordered one online. I am quite the procrastinator for things like this. So, one day in May, the package arrived, and I told Jay "I bought a magnetic screen door," expecting him to be surprised.

Turns out he had been doing some research too and he thought maybe a sliding door is better and he also had gone out to get one, unbeknownst to me! He thought a sliding door would not be "too hard" to put in. I thought that was a matter of opinion but was happy for Jay to try.

We used to have this joke about renewing our 'lesbian membership card' whenever we did something handy around the house. It was funny before Jay came out as trans. Now, I wasn't sure if it would still be funny. I paused with the joke on the tip of my tongue. It felt like a loss that I needed to think about what to say. I never felt like I needed to do that before in our relationship, but now I felt like I needed to think carefully. The last thing I wanted to do was hurt Jay. I missed our old joke but did not like second guessing myself. Still, I kept on thinking about whether to crack that old joke about the membership card. It used to be our thing, but I worried how it would land now.

I decided to go for it.

"I guess you won't need to renew your lesbian membership card anymore," I said.

He laughed, and so did I, as relief washed over me. The joke went over just fine. Phew!

In the end, we tried the magnetic door first. The cat ran right through the magnetic closing. It kept out the mosquitos but wouldn't keep the cat safe from the neighborhood's resident coyotes. Jay then tried to install the sliding door. It was harder than he thought! Though throughout the struggle, I kept on giggling on the inside about the expired membership card. I thought maybe I could find Jay an actual "Trans membership card" to replace his old metaphorical one just for fun.

In the end, we called a handyperson who installed the sliding screen door in no time. Some things are just too complicated!

Then, it was Mother's Day. Prior to the transition, I always thought of Mother's Day as the "lesbian holiday." We both got to celebrate being moms at the same time! I was apprehensive about how this first Mother's Day in our transitioning family would feel.

Prior to realizing he was trans, Jay would often participate in the "Run Like a Mother" race in the morning. Some years, the kids and I went to the race and made lots of signs for Jay to cheer him on. The morning of the race, we would have brunch and make lots of cards. I would help the kids make cards for Jay. He would help the kids make cards for me. It was a full-day celebration and a big day for everyone.

After running by himself for a few years, my mom, Jay,

and I went and took part in the race. That year, Jay ran on his own ahead of us and even placed for time and age. He is a much faster runner than the rest of us, having run competitively in high school and college. But that year we walked and jogged for fun without him. We still got the participation medal and T-shirt.

While I enjoyed these Mother's Days, they were stressful for Jay. Perhaps the running was a way for him to release some unconscious tension about a day that celebrated motherhood. What I do know is he wanted the day to be special for me and felt that sharing the day meant that neither one of us really got to be treated to the honor of the day. On some level, I think I might have had similar feelings, but for a different reason.

A perfect Mother's Day for me would never involve waking up early to go for a run. Running is something Jay loves. If I were to create a day just for me, it would involve sleeping in, having a nice family brunch with pastries at home, and doing something fun and relaxing with the kids. Maybe it would include going on a walk or a hike in the woods. The races on Mother's Days were a compromise, so we each had something we loved to do. I got my brunch, and he got his race.

Of course, now I understand on a different level why a day called Mother's Day never sat well with him. Perhaps running on these days was more than exercise. Running could have been a way to relieve the mounting unconscious stress the day brought on. But, since neither of us realized that for years, it was the best way for us both to be happy. I also think part of what made it hard was that Jay knew he should feel special, and that piled on the pressure.

But that first Mother's Day after Jay's coming out as trans ended up being the type of day I would have created, had it just been for me all along. We decided no one would be racing this day!

Jay bought me some beautiful flowers. He woke up early and went to my favorite local bakery and brought back some pastries to share. We had brunch with strawberries, raspberries, pastries, and eggs.

The day was beautiful. It was sunny, but not too hot. We spent some of the day in the backyard enjoying the chirping birds and spring flowers. We have a rhododendron bush that goes the length of our backyard, and it was bursting with purple, pink, and reddish flowers.

For my Mother's Day gift, the kids and Jay built me a raised garden bed in our backyard. We would plant lettuce and kale along with sugar snap peas. Later, during the summer, we planted tomatoes, basil, and peppers.

As special as the day had been, this holiday was still a challenging one for me. During that first Mother's Day, I had a lot of big feelings to deal with. On the one hand, I was happy for Jay to get his own day. He would get Father's Day for the first time, and that was really exciting. On the other hand, I missed having this shared and particularly lesbian holiday experience with him.

Even though everyone had worked so hard to make the day amazingly wonderful, I still had some moments of "the feels." There was a while (probably about an hour) in the afternoon when I felt waves of sadness wash over me.

Chapter 7

Before working with a therapist, I probably would have tried to put away the feelings and not let myself experience them. I would have been so afraid that they would stick around that I would stuff them down, being the one to cause them to stick around and linger.

So instead of avoiding and denying them, I sat on the front porch and grieved over the loss of what Mother's Day used to be like. Even though this day couldn't have been better for me, I still felt this loss and sadness. This wasn't the Mother's Day I could have anticipated a year ago. Jay saw me and asked me what was up. There was a part of me that didn't want to share how I was feeling. But I dug deep inside and found the bravery to be fully honest about my feelings. He sat there and genuinely listened. I'm sure my sadness and grief were hard for him to hear, but they were the truth. Feeling like I could share these deep feelings, that honestly, I was ashamed of having, made me feel seen and loved just as much, or maybe even more than the flowers and gifts had. Part of me felt guilty about having these feelings, and I wished I could wholeheartedly accept this change without having negative feelings. I had this idea that the perfect partner would just be happy for their spouse and get over their sad feelings immediately. Why did I have to feel this way? Why couldn't I just be purely happy with every step of the journey? Of course, I was happy for Jay, but I also had feelings about how things had changed.

I am not a big fan of change. For example, my spouse has been attempting to convince me to change the color of paint in our kitchen for 6 years and it only happened because we had a massive flood and it had to be repainted, anyway. I find change stressful and difficult, even changes in mundane details, like which shoes I wear—the same pair, but new versions of it for the past I don't know how many years—to life-altering changes. I like physical things in my environment to remain stable. Jay's transition was a lot more impactful on me than a new pair of shoes or a new color for the kitchen walls. I find change overwhelming, scary, and something to be avoided, especially when I'm not the one initiating the change.

Looking back, I see how I had two strong conflicting sets of beliefs that made this new Mother's Day tradition more difficult. I don't like change and wanted nothing to change because I had wonderful memories of how the holiday used to be—sometimes running a race, sometimes spending the day with my mom, and sometimes celebrating womanhood and motherhood with Jay. Still, I loved the way this new day was shaping up. It was wonderful. The strawberries we planted in the new raised bed that Jay and the kids built me were exciting to look at. The brunch, sleep in time, and having a day being pampered were all amazing experiences. But the only way I could embrace the day fully was also acknowledging that there was sadness around the change.

Thankfully, I had been consistent with therapy since January and had lots of experience of not stepping into my old patterns. I had a whole life of trying to avoid feelings of sadness, anger, or anything that was negative in my mind. But now, instead of pushing them down and denying their existence, I let Jay know I needed some time to acknowledge my feelings about the new way Mother's Day was this year. I had gone out to the front porch so he wouldn't have to experience my sadness.

While sitting on the porch, Jay went way above and beyond in the sense that he was deeply involved in why I was sad. He was able to put away his personal feelings (which must have been intense) about how I was feeling grief on this day, when he had done everything to make it wonderful for me. He did not take it personally. He put his arm around my shoulder and let me have my feelings without trying to fix them. I felt better and could embrace all this new Mother's Day offered.

Even after my feelings moved on, I would still get echoes. I would be in the new (more positive) mood and then I would get a small echo of how I was feeling, then I would go back to the new feeling. But even while that was happening, I could get back into enjoying this new way of celebrating Mother's Day. In the end, the day was glorious. Different, and not anything I could have expected, but still wonderful.

How is it for me a few years after that first Mother's Day?

It has taken some time, but now I don't have those mixed feelings about the day. It really is amazing, but I enjoy the holiday more than I did before. Maybe it is the kids getting older and so getting to really sleep in is a reality for both of us. Maybe it is that I'm not just used to things but have come to the place where I wouldn't wish my life to be different. I'm not sure when that happened, but at some point, I realized I am grateful that Jay realized he was trans and wouldn't wish anything different from how it is. No matter the reason, time has helped tremendously. I now look forward to each Mother's Day with no sense of mixed feelings.

Knowing what I do now, I'm happy that Jay doesn't have to share this day with me. I'm thrilled that he gets his own day. He no longer has a sense of not fitting. I get to enjoy the day my way.

This past year I had a moment, after Mother's Day had passed, when I realized - *Wow. I didn't think about how it used to be at all.* There were no echoes of the past in my memories; just the day at hand to celebrate. I wished I could go back and tell myself during that first year of transition, there will be a time when this won't be a big deal. I also wish I could tell myself you don't need to feel guilty about having feelings. Of course, you have strong feelings about things changing. Hello! You have a strong "automatic no" reaction when Jay suggests we rearrange the furniture in the guest room. There will be a time when we both will be celebrated by the people we love in the way we want to be loved. I would also tell myself it is totally okay to have all the feelings you are having. You do not have to feel guilty. The sadness is partly about how much you love Jay, and it is normal. Just let yourself have those feelings and then trust that it will all work out in its own way. You won't be able to control the outcome, but trust that you can not only handle it, but you will be more than okay.

Chapter 8

June

Summer vacation arrived, bringing a flurry of events. Our daughter Liz was born in the middle of June and on top of that, Jay has his birthday in June. Father's Day was always celebrated with our kids' biological dad, and sometimes Jay's father and my father were there too. Talk about a few busy days of family, love, and celebration. (And crazy full days of cooking two cakes, having two or three events in a few days and massive socializing—which is a lot for introverted me to handle!)

This June, though, would be the first of its kind. Jay would get to celebrate his first Father's Day! Not only that, but he would also celebrate his first birthday, as himself.

The kids call their bio-dad Apa. (A nickname for Father in Spanish and the name he called his father.) Often there would be a Pride Parade on Father's Day, and so our family would go downtown to watch and return for a BBQ after.

We are very close to the kid's Apa and have dinner with him almost every Sunday as well. Jay and I don't have parents in town. I've actually been friends with the kid's Apa longer than I've known Jay! Over time, he moved from being a friend to part of our family who comes to most of our major holiday celebrations like Thanksgiving and Christmas and is accepted by our extended families. We used to joke around that we were Apa's sister wives. (No, we don't have *that* type of relationship. He is as gay as can be!)

I wanted both celebrations to be special for Jay, but I wasn't sure how the kids' biological dad would feel about sharing Father's Day. Would that be strange to him? Would it be awkward for all of us?

Both Jay and I were apprehensive about how Apa would feel about sharing Father's Day with Jay. Apa had been great about the transition and was so supportive of both of us. We figured it would go okay. But it would still be an enormous shift for all of us. The kids would go from having one father and two mothers to . . . two fathers and one mother!

On occasions, I thought, so do I now have brother husbands? I think we might just qualify as Fox News' ideas of a nightmare! But our family is full of love and acceptance and what can be better than that?

Apa and Jay discussed it and, as a family, we all decided that we still wanted to go to the Pride Parade. Apa participated in the parade with a social group he belongs to. We watched him and all the other floats go along the streets, cheering them on.

Chapter 8

Little did we know, next year COVID would hit, and it would be a while until we would get to attend that parade again as a family. My parents were visiting that year and came along for the celebrations, along with Jay's brother and wife and their oldest and only child at the time. In retrospect, I am even more thankful that we all went and shared that experience before so many things changed for a few years.

I had a moment at the parade when I wondered how people viewed me. Even though I know intellectually, no one was spending any brain power thinking about me, I still had a busy mind. Do people think we are a straight couple watching the parade? Do they think one of our kids is queer and we are being supportive of them? I wanted a sign or shirt that showed I was still part of the community. Maybe we need a flag of our own?

It was still easy to knock me off my balance emotionally at this time, but the feelings didn't overwhelm me. They were more like an annoying gnat I had to ignore and choose to shift my focus back on the excitement and joy all around me.

Some highlights of the parade were catching fabulous rainbow face paint markers tossed by people from one float, hanging out with the therapy llama, and seeing my niece so excited about all the floats.

After the Pride Parade, we went home to celebrate Jay's birthday! I and lots of other people gave him "It's a Boy" type of birthday cards. Guests came over to our house for a nice outdoor celebration. Surrounded by so many friends, I felt so loved and supported. We were being accepted by our community. People were not only accepting of Jay, but of our relationship and family. Going into summer, we were surrounded by people who meant the most to us. Our immediate family and those who accepted and embraced us, no matter what.

CHAPTER 9

JULY

Once Jay started questioning his identity, I knew he would want top surgery. So many memories came to the front of my mind and clicked into place. One particular memory made total sense now. For years, Jay had wished he had some excuse to get rid of his breasts. Knowing many dear friends and some family members who have had cancer and needed to have surgery for that reason, I wouldn't wish that upon him or anyone. He even entertained thoughts of cancer, though he would never wish that on anyone or our family. But it was how he felt, and because of this, I knew immediately after he questioned his identity that this would be in our future. I did not know at the time if he would identify as non-binary or trans. I also did not know if he would want testosterone or not. (At first, he said he was not interested.) But top surgery was a foregone conclusion in my mind.

Despite knowing immediately, Jay had to wait until a

certain amount of time passed by before he would qualify for surgery. Because he was an adult and actually had a long history of wanting this, that would speed up the process. Also, the fact that I have health insurance by working as a public employee in a more liberal state meant that the surgery would be covered once it was approved by insurance!

Jay and I went to his very first top surgery consultation. While on the one hand, I was apprehensive about this next medical step, mostly, I just wanted to have it done and over with. We parked and took the elevator up to the office. Waiting to be called back, we sat next to each other in the waiting room. What do you talk about when in the waiting room before a consultation like this? I think I found a travel magazine and looked at it. After not that long, we were both called back.

Jay filled out a bunch of forms and then the doctor walked into the room and introduced herself. She looked over Jay's history and quickly zeroed in that he had been on testosterone for less than 6 months. She began a barrage of questions about his reason for wanting the surgery so soon during the transitioning period. Immediately after he came out as questioning his gender, Jay started wearing a sports bra almost all the time. This included when we were intimate. This meant that the last time I intimately interacted with his boobs was before I knew, and suddenly they were out of the repertoire. While I understood on an intellectual level that this was important to him, there were moments when this was very hard for me. The sudden change that I wasn't expecting didn't give me a sense of

Chapter 9

closure. One day, the chest was okay and the next it was off the menu. I could roll with these changes a little easier as I realized how much more comfortable Jay was with his body this way. I had a myriad of feelings, many of which I had a hard time even describing or discussing with him. But when the surgeon questioned if Jay was absolutely sure about top surgery, I knew I needed to speak up for him.

While Jay was only recently aware of being trans, I shared with the doctor that he had wanted to remove his breasts for years. The only time he had appreciated having boobs was when he was breastfeeding, which was a time long past. I felt protective of Jay. I understood the surgeon wanted to make sure Jay had thought this out, but he was accompanied by his supportive wife of eighteen years and mother to their three children. This wasn't a split-moment decision.

During the visit, the doctor explained that since the surgery center was located in a hospital connected with the Catholic Church, she would need approval to do the surgery. First, she would have to go to the review board and present the case for surgery. The doctor didn't believe Jay's case would pass because they required people to be on hormone replacement therapy for at least one year prior to surgery. However, doing the surgery at a different hospital might be a possibility.

Either way, even though the doctor was just doing her job, it was clear to both of us after we left, she was not the right fit for us. I remember leaving that appointment feeling icky. It didn't feel great to be questioned, even though it wasn't me being questioned. It just felt wrong. And considering Jay had worked with a social worker, been approved for testosterone and continued to do therapy, we felt he was well prepared to make this decision. The way she handled our appointment made it clear in the end that she was not the right surgeon for us.

From there, Jay attended the next two consultations on his own with doctors who were both understanding and professional. In the end, we went with a doctor who was in my health insurance network. It took much longer to get the appointment, but it was worth the wait. She treated Jay with respect and let him know that in September or October, he would get a call to schedule his surgery. The plan was set.

Now we waited.

Chapter 10

August

Later in the summer, we traveled out of state for a family reunion. This would be the first time we saw more of our relatives. We met in a rural logging community where some of our relatives live. Most of Jay's extended family made the trip from the East Coast and a few other states. I was nervous about how meeting the relatives (cousins and aunts and uncles) would turn out. I was also anxious (Jay probably way more than me) about how people in the community would take his transition. Jay had worked in the small town two different summers and spent a lot of his summers there when growing up in the community.

One branch of the family did not have a history of being overly supportive of us. This was the branch of the family that lived and worked there. They were always polite to our faces but would not come to our original wedding. (We didn't invite them to any more of our marriage celebrations after that.) They did not believe that gay relationships were to be accepted, especially given some books they shared with my mother-in-law. If gay relationships were not acceptable, I couldn't imagine they would be okay with my spouse transitioning. Still, they had always been kind to us and nice to our children, so it was hard to know how this visit with them in their rural community would go.

No one was mean or rude to our faces. People in the community who he had worked with previously were all kind and accepting. Things were definitely awkward with one branch of the family, but there were enough of us there to mostly avoid them. It was easier to do in a large group of people I enjoyed spending time with. After the reunion, though, one particular cousin sent a very long, detailed email explaining why they were not okay with Jay transitioning. It's likely the entire branch of the family felt similarly.

The cousin used a significant part of the letter to argue that "many people" who transition later regret their decision and find out that they were mistaken. The cousin felt he needed to let us know he was not ok with Jay's transition and that he must question our choices. He said that the questioning was done out of love for Jay and concern that Jay was making a big mistake. The letter described how gender is purely biological and argued many other points that don't deserve to be repeated here.

Both Jay and I had some additional thoughts about the letter. This particular cousin has these nicely manicured long nails. I don't think they are ever polished, but they clearly get buffed and treated carefully. His mannerisms also are not typical for a rural guy. We are all for gender expression. Truly, I say be you, be your own fabulous self! As long as you are not hurting other people, go for it. Jay and I have wondered on more than one occasion if this cousin was jealous of Jay's transition, even if unaware of his feelings. Maybe that is why he was so bothered by the whole situation. It is easier to have some compassion for his cousin. Maybe what he wrote to us is really what he had been saying to himself, not that we could ask him that.

Honestly, rereading his email while I was writing this book made my stomach churn. It created a bit of a panic response in me. My chest felt hot and heavy, and my body felt awful all over. The letter added to our complex feelings about this part of the family for not coming to our wedding. They clearly never approved of us for so many years already. The letter made us wonder more about how they really felt about us before. I wondered if they had all discussed the contents before sending it. Was the cousin just the spokesperson for them all? I wasn't curious enough to ask. I had the good sense to realize that knowing more would not be helpful.

In the end, I feel like if you do not have a relationship where you know my favorite colors, my favorite hobbies or interests, you definitely do not know enough about me to question my identity or my spouse's identity, for that matter. While I don't mind if people ask open-ended questions—ideally directed to me and not my spouse—there is a difference between a genuine conversation and being asked to justify who he and I feel like at our core. Jay is not any more required to explain how he views his sense of identity to anyone any more than a cis person should have to explain theirs. And he definitely does not need to justify himself to cousins and relatives who skipped our wedding.

Jay graciously wrote a response to this email. I think the words that trigger a nauseating response in me aren't so much from the cousin's letter, but also that other family members could not understand how hurtful the letter felt to us. Unfortunately, Jay's immediate family mostly gave excuses for his cousin instead of empathizing with how Jay and I might feel about receiving the letter. I wish they could have centered their response around first supporting us instead of excusing hurtful behavior, no matter how "well intentioned" the letter was. There is this saying about good intentions...

Some comments we heard.

- "They were well meaning."
- "They didn't mean to hurt you."
- "They were just trying to be helpful."

This is NOT what it means to be an ally. Being an ally means supporting the person who is transitioning. Being an ally looks like taking those questions to experts or to people outside of the person who is transitioning.

If you have people in your life who are not supportive of you, or say hurtful things, please know you are not alone. You are strong. You have got this. You are loved and your feelings and identity are valid. You do not need to explain your family, love, or relationship to anyone. You deserve to be supported with unconditional love. Sadly, not all humans will rise to the occasion. Please do what you need to take care of yourself.

My heart goes out to you if you are experiencing unsupportive family members, friends, and conversations. You will get through it. Life will get better. The memory will always be there in your mind, but over time, you will revisit the memory with less and less frequency. One day, you might even forget to think about it. That change is the beginning of healing.

One day, you hopefully will see the experience with a sense of humor. Humor is the best medicine in my mind. Please know that those who would like to tear you down are clearly dealing with their own unresolved issues. They are confined in a rigid box in their own mind. I do not wish them any ill. But I will not tolerate a lack of respect for my spouse or children, or me.

One of the biggest blessings of COVID for me was not seeing this cousin or that side of our extended family for a solid two years. This last year, they actually came to the family reunion, and we honestly had an enjoyable time. Our kids know about the history, and yet we were all able to find some common ground and enjoy hanging out. We were once again in a more rural part (of our state this time) and we did some awesome star watching at night. We, of course, avoided any conflict, but funny how sweeping things under the rug sometimes works. (Though not in intimate relationships!) This distance has allowed for some healing for me and my immediate family.

The first time I started writing this section and rereading the letters, it was profoundly difficult for me. I ended up needing to take some time to release these feelings. I started by sitting in a rocking chair—the same rocking chair where I was nursed as a baby. I rocked back and forth and put my hands over my chest. It was pouring outside, so I just allowed the tears to flow down my face as I listened to the rain pouring down from above. I let myself feel the grief that I had blocked for so long.

I don't think I had ever really cried or grieved this rejection before. At the time, I was so focused on taking care of Jay and supporting him that I put my own needs on the back burner. So, I just rocked, looked out at the sky, and let my feelings release.

After some time, the tears subsided. I felt a little shaky, but that didn't bother me. I know that shakiness is simply how I feel after this type of experience. My stomach felt nauseous. I then decided what I really needed more than anything else was to get into bed. I turned on some lullabies for sleep and got under an extra soft blanket. Lying down, I breathed deeply and tried to relax, but my thoughts were rushing. One useful thought I had among the flurry of them was that I would enjoy snuggling with Bubbles, our coming out dog. I needed her at this moment.

I found Bubbles lying down next to our youngest daughter, Joan, and asked to borrow her for some time. Bubbles immediately laid down next to me for cuddling. Before I knew it, I awoke with Bubbles lying on my feet. I felt much better, still a little raw, but strong and okay at the same time.

Chapter 10

The next day, I continued to take care of myself. I was still feeling nauseous from my thoughts and from re-experiencing the painful emotions. I took an early morning walk around the neighborhood before the sun came up.

After I did my normal morning routine of waking up Joan and reading the *Babysitters Club* book with her as she ate an enchilada, I woke up Liz. I sat next to Liz on the bed and rubbed her back gently to wake her up. I also talked for a minute with my son Cole about his plans for the day, something I do many mornings before I head off to work.

Last, before I left, I did a guided meditation found on YouTube. I can't actually visualize anything in my head, so I repeat the words I hear like an echo. That helps me have a task to do.

After the meditation, I felt much calmer. I wish I had learned these strategies earlier in the transition, but honestly, it took me years to learn.

While some people are very upfront about their disapproval, others quietly quit our friendships. That can be a lot harder to read. Have they really gotten busy? Are we drifting apart, or is their silence about something else? Looking back, both Jay and I can see that quite a few people who "accepted" us have drifted out of our lives. Yes, they sent nice emails, but they stopped inviting us over to their house for BBQs or social and family gatherings. Our perspective on this now is twofold. First, what in the world? They were okay with us as a lesbian couple, but not as a straight appearing couple. That's both strange and messed up! And a little hilarious at the same time. Our second general perspective on this is that maybe they weren't as good of friends as we thought. Friendship is a choice, and we choose now to hang out with people who really love us no matter what. The people who have stuck with us for the long run, though, we know truly love and accept us no matter what.

It would have been nice to know who was really going to be supportive, especially in the months that came up. It also would have been helpful to have some effective techniques for dealing with overwhelming feelings. That would have been helpful for me, especially in the lead-up to Ryan's top surgery.

That is where I am taking you next.

Chapter 11

September

On my first day back to work after summer vacation, I found out that Jay had a surgery date. But before this call came in, the day began with some high anxiety.

I woke up around 5 am with physical discomfort. Having worked with a therapist about this ailment for multiple years, I tried my toolbox. I took deep breaths. I reminded myself that this discomfort was a physical sensation but meant nothing. I reframed my thoughts, saying, "I'm just really excited for the day! This feeling is just excitement." I reminded myself that I was feeling my brain's habitual electrical patterns. I recollected I feel this every year and I am actually a skilled teacher with high achieving results. I remind myself that I was chosen to coach other teachers because I am good at what I do. Then I tried a mindfulness and acceptance meditation.

None of it worked.

I just couldn't accept my feelings, and eventually, I had to give up and get ready to go to work, regardless of the anxiety.

The stress around "Back to School" and work comes in part from the many "get to know you again" activities. They are my idea of hell. I am sensitive to noise and often find social chit-chat uncomfortable and confusing. Icebreakers are the worst for me. I can't prepare as I'm driving in to work for the questions that will be asked. Normally I prepare for the "how was your weekend" questions on my drive to work on Monday. But with icebreakers, the leader might ask anything from, "If your life was a song, what would the title be?" to "What color do you feel best represents how you feel about coming back to work? And why?" Everyone is talking at once, so it is loud. People stand close to each other so they can talk in groups. I have to figure out who to stand next to and prepare myself for anything. These gatherings are an overwhelming way to start back up the year.

This year the question was, "Name a favorite book." I read so many books every summer, so to think of a favorite seemed impossible. When my mind is in an anxious state, I am flooded with racing thoughts in my head. Should I share something that I read for pleasure over the summer that is not related to work? Will it seem "uncool" to share that the book I enjoyed the most was something technical and related to my job? While I'm stewing with my thoughts, I'm not being a superb listener to my colleagues and friends during their responses.

Chapter 11

My mind goes into a loop. *"I don't know what to say. I don't have any ideas. What books do I like to read? I can't come up with anything. I should look in my Kindle book list or library book app and choose from one of the 248 books listed there. Which ones did I read this summer? Which one is my favorite? I can't take out the library app right now. Damn. I'm supposed to be listening to other people. I need to find an idea that is light and neutral. I hate this. I don't know what to say."* And my mind circles over and over until I finally talk and get that conversation over with.

To avoid this, if I can manage, the best thing I can do in these situations is answer quickly, so I'm not ruminating on what I am going to say. But then, after I share, sometimes my inner voice spouts judgmental things about how my answer wasn't good enough. I don't really get to know other people better in these types of situations because I am fighting against listening to my inner voice, which is loudly sharing a million ideas a minute at me.

First days back after summer vacation, also consist of breakfast and lunch. What's wrong with that? Well, first, I am so nauseous I can't eat. But also, so anxious I want to eat so I don't have to talk. I hate figuring out where to sit. Who do I sit next to? And then the uplifting breakfast music is playing, to add to the sensory experience.

Within ten minutes of arriving, I was ready to retreat into my private space, but I didn't have keys to my room yet. They aren't handed out until after the "office talk" where we learn, again, how to make a copy and are reminded about not fixing machines when they inevitably break. Honestly, all I want to do is connect individually with my colleagues, friends, and any new teachers I'm coaching, not in a group setting.

Midway through the morning, our new vice-principal introduced herself to us and brought us outside to do a team-building exercise. In that exercise, we were supposed to hold pieces of yarn and make a net. Then one by one she had colleagues drop their piece of yarn to show what happens when one of us doesn't pull our own weight. She explained how we needed to do better and lectured us about not dropping our strings. I think the message was supposed to be uplifting, but my brain was not processing it that way. Whether she meant it or not, I felt attacked. The whole day started out on the wrong foot.

Soon after that, it was time to eat lunch together, which was thoughtfully provided, but left no time to relax or refresh before the afternoon. Now, knowing more about how to take care of myself, I would have gone for a walk and listened to music in headphones or done something else to self-soothe. I desperately needed to recharge from all the social interaction of the morning, but I didn't feel capable of advocating for myself. I also didn't have a large toolbox of coping tools. I doubled down and tried reframing my thoughts, being social, pushing through my anxiety, and being a "good team player."

Immediately following lunch, we had training on what to do in the aftermath of a school shooting. This brought up memories of a previous lockdown where we believed there was a bomb in the school. My room was a direct line from the main entrance door and because of the timing of

Chapter 11

everything, I ended up with my 25 elementary students and at least 30 more terrified middle schoolers. I still vividly remember a middle schooler asking me if they were going to live as I saw the flashing lights from the police vehicles through the pulled down shades. My room looked out over the parking lot, which was getting a lot of police action. I knew nothing about what was happening, just that it was clearly not a drill. I texted Jay to say I loved him and the family once I got the students settled with some paper to draw on and told the middle schoolers to please feel free to text their families. I reminded them to first double check that everything really was on silent.

On that first day back to work, sitting in the stifling hot basement library, I learned all about how to "Stop the Bleed," (Um. . . how about banning automatic guns and having permits like for driving a car? It's a little late to try to stop the bleed after gunshot wounds have occurred.)

The heat of the day, my anxiety all combined with the topic, made me even more uncomfortable. We watched graphic videos and had to practice how to stuff wounds on manikins. It was stomach turning. It was during this training, after everything I had gone through that morning, that Jay's text came in.

Surgery scheduled for November!

It was the call Jay had been waiting for.

Sitting at the back round table, already feeling my heart pounding from the gory topic at hand, I felt numb. "Oh, my gosh. It's happening. It's really happening," I thought.

I was excited for Jay. I replied with a heart emoji and

texted something supportive, then tried to focus on how to dress wounds getting through the rest of the day.

Soon after those first few days back to school, I descended further into major anxiety melt-down mode. To be fair, this happens at the beginning of the school year almost every year. So, it was hard for me to know how much of it was Jay's transition vs. the normal aspect of me having my yearly beginning-of-the-school-year panic attacks. But anticipating surgery didn't help me.

Every morning, I woke up with my pulse racing, my body sweating, and my thoughts rushing. I tried to tell myself I can handle this. I listened to a meditation. I tried to eat but had no appetite. I couldn't brush my teeth in the morning without gagging.

In previous years, this would happen, but once at school and teaching, it would be like a switch went off. I just had to get through 4:30 am until 8 am. The moment students walked through the door, my anxiety would go away. And every morning I would remind myself that I was going to feel just fine.

This year, though, the anxiety didn't go away. I was coaching and only teaching a few Spanish classes a week. I didn't have the switch off that used to turn off as I went into my teacher mode. Even while at work, my heart raced. I was sweating and barely functioning. I was the "dropped string" in the web that my vice-principal talked about the first day back. I felt horribly guilty about how I wasn't pulling my own weight. I started bringing a change of clothes to school every day because I was sweating through the first set. I knew I needed help.

Chapter 11

I couldn't get in to see my doctor, so I eventually ended up at Urgent Care, needing something to help me with my anxiety. I was offered something like a Benadryl. That made me sleepy and more anxious. Later, I was given a referral to a psychiatrist and a beta blocker while I waited for that appointment. The beta blocker did not help, and there were no psychiatrist appointments available for weeks. Finally, the psychiatrist added a new SSRI to the antidepressant I was already on. I really needed something to stop the spiraling three weeks ago, not something that might help in three more weeks.

During my lunch break, sometimes I would lie down on the ground in my room and try to do a progressive meditation. Really, nothing gave me relief. I don't think I had ever experienced this level of unresolved anxiety before.

I was also barely functioning at home. It took all my energy just to get through each day at school, and I had very little to give to our three children and Jay. I felt awful but was in survival mode and barely surviving.

Jay worried my anxiety was because of the surgery and his transition. I think the major anxiety had to do with the loading up of multiple factors and not having effective self-soothing skills to handle these emotions. Tapping was helpful, but I needed something a lot stronger to deal with my circumstances.

The new vice-principal was very direct and critical, which is not something I handled well at all. I had a different teaching schedule that did not offer me a first period block with students every day. In the past, my classroom of students helped me snap back to being calm and focused. I was anxious about the surgery. I was stuck in a terrible pattern of anxiety and couldn't free myself from it, no matter what I tried. I was worried about what was going to happen after the surgery. What if I was still a mess? Would I be able to care for our three children and my spouse? I could barely take care of myself.

There was no way I was going to ask Jay to postpone the surgery, but I had serious doubts about my ability to cope and handle everything. I needed help but wasn't sure where to turn. While Jay had a clear path forward and a plan, I felt like I was zigzagging all over the place with a malfunctioning GPS system.

Eventually, I realized I needed to reach out to my mom and let her know just how poorly I was doing. She had experienced major depression herself as well in her work as a Nurse Practitioner specializing in people's complex mental health needs. While she was now retired, she had a wealth of knowledge ready for me when I finally let her know what was going on. She immediately understood that I needed more support than I was getting. She explained to me and Jay that I needed a different class of medication. She helped me contact my primary care doctor to get an anti-anxiety medicine that would help calm down the fight-or-flight response. In the end, it was my primary care doctor and my mom, not the psychiatrist, that was the most helpful. My mom also made a plan to come up and stay with me for at least three weeks after the surgery so I would have the support I clearly needed with the daily

Chapter 11

tasks of running the household. Plans were being put into place for all of us. Jay had a plan. My mom had a plan. All I had was anxiety, but now the start of a plan.

Plans are important in this process, so no one is left behind.

CHAPTER 12

OCTOBER

One month before the surgery was filled with preparation. Jay would have to be extremely cautious after the procedure to not use his arms or risk stretching the scars. That meant I would need to step up to help more when I was already struggling. I had lots of nervous energy and was a wreck, feeling like I was failing miserably at being a wife and parent. I had no place to direct all this energy. It felt shameful to share the truth about being overwhelmed with taking care of three children and Jay after surgery, so I stuffed my feelings down.

I tried to put on a brave face at work and prayed no one walked into my office during the many panic attacks. I would literally lie on the floor trying to talk myself down while hiding behind a curtain. I felt guilty that I wasn't doing more around the house and helping Jay with the chores. I tried to keep things together for the kids and somehow managed to put on a happy face for them. I hoped so anyway.

My emotions were not constant. Just like my thoughts were a swirling whirlwind, my emotions had their own circus going on. Some moments I was joyful and so happy for Jay. At other times, I was in the depths of despair. The fluctuating ups and downs of my feelings were so hard to deal with for both me and Jay. And I really wasn't fooling Jay with my happy face.

Jay knows my moods better than anyone. He could tell that I was struggling. He knew I was waking up with panic attacks every morning and could see the changes of clothes I was bringing to work. He knew I needed help and encouraged me to reach out for more professional support.

I continued to attend my spouse's group, but I also started going to an individual counselor. Private counseling helped me put a plan in place for how I was going to approach the surgery and recovery period and beyond.

I found this therapist through another person who had a trans spouse. Arriving the first day, I wasn't sure what to expect. She was a holistic therapist, and I had no clue what that meant.

I wasn't looking for a "high success rate." I just wanted a therapist who I would not need to educate on what it meant to have a trans spouse. Other people with trans spouses online and in other places had so many stories to tell about needing to educate their therapist. Some therapists weren't clear on the differences between gender or sexuality. Some even suggested that the non-transitioning spouse leave the relationship, saying most couples don't survive the transition.

My priority was finding someone warm and supportive during this vulnerable time. I needed a therapist who supported people in their transitions. This recommended therapist gave me this and so much more.

The therapist had her office in her house with a beautiful garden surrounding it. Her office had a massage table, a comfortable couch, and lots of plants. I have loved plants since I was a child. Plants are one of my most consistent companions over the years. In 4th grade, I got my first mini terrarium as a birthday present. I would grow plants, do experiments to see if they responded to different music styles played in our basement on an old record player. I had an entire table of plants by the age of 10 that I would talk to. Even today, I have a plethora of hanging plants on the wall in the bathroom. So, walking into the therapist's office, which was inundated by beautiful tropical lush green leaves, I felt at home. This was not the clinical setting of my previous therapy sessions.

I remember sitting down on the couch, taking off my shoes, and tucking my feet up beside me on the couch. This is how I calm myself. Even in the car, I always take off my shoes, which drives Jay insane. The problem isn't the smell. It's that when it's time to get out of the car, I don't have my shoes on yet. I try to remember to put them on a few minutes before we arrive at a place but can still forget. So, the first thing I did to get comfortable with therapy was take off my shoes after checking with the therapist that she didn't mind. There is something comforting about being on a couch with my legs pulled in tight and without shoes on my feet. If I was going to learn to talk about all my various emotions, I would need to be physically comfortable.

In counseling, we started by working on calming my nervous system. It was really unlike any counseling I had done in the past. Previously, I had sought help for my depression and anxiety with both Acceptance and Commitment Therapy (ACT) and Cognitive Behavioral Therapy (CBT). In both methods, I spent a lot of the sessions talking about my thoughts, labeling the thoughts, and then coming up with alternate thoughts. For example, I might say: I'm feeling anxious about how I will feel when Jay no longer has boobs and sad about that. Then the counselor would help me label the thought. I learned this statement was called fortune telling as I was trying to expect how I would feel in the future. Then the counselor would work with me to create a more positive statement about the future, like: I don't know how I'll feel when Jay's boobs are gone, but I trust that I will be able to handle it.

The counselor I was working with had a totally different way of working than my past therapies. We would talk for a little while, and then she would ask me where I am feeling the emotions in my body. We would pause. She would have me place my hand on my belly and breath into the spot, holding the emotion. Other times I would lie on a massage table fully clothed, and she would hold my feet or head while staying with the emotion. There was a lot less talking and more experiencing the feelings without pushing them away. The counselor would

Chapter 12

notice when I went into my head and would bring me back to my body. She would say, "It is safe. You don't have to push down and away what you are feeling." She helped me get more in touch with my feelings and taught me to sit through my sadness, where I found deeper peace and acceptance. Instead of speaking words to change how I was feeling, I accepted my feelings and allowed them to resolve naturally. I left each session with a sense of calm and feeling grounded. Instead of words like, "I know I can handle this," I felt centered and steady. Even if those feelings didn't last for long after, during the session, this therapy gave me a reprieve amid all my worries.

The counselor also helped me with making a plan of my own. I told her how worried I was about taking care of the kids and Jay and gave her the details about the actual day of the surgery. I opened up about my fears, knowing that I wouldn't be hurting anyone's feelings in that space with her. It wasn't an easy thing for me to do. Even telling this neutral person about my fears was scary. But the risk was worth it. I left there with my own plan.

With the therapist's guidance, I made a complete plan on how to care for myself before, during, and after the surgery. Before the surgery, I learned I needed more help. Given my mental state and overwhelm, I was glad my mom was coming to stay with us for three weeks. She would be with us between the surgery and through Thanksgiving. Knowing that I was going to have an adult in the house who would help me with everything changed my outlook. I felt calmer already. As a bonus, my mom is a retired medical professional, so having someone who could help with any of the aftercare was a tremendous help. Mostly, though, she offered to support me by driving all three children to and from school and being around the house if I needed to assist Jay.

Preparing for Surgery

You probably will want some level of emotional support. Here are some questions to ask yourself:

- Who are people you can lean on and feel comfortable talking about the full range of your emotions? If the honest answer is that you do not have anyone, here are some ideas:
- There are secret Facebook groups you can join. You need to search and apply, but they exist.
- Forums like Reddit and other spaces where you can post anonymously. Please be careful, but you can find valuable advice in these places.
- The appendix in this book focuses on forming a network with other trans spouses. Please take a look for ideas.

- Look for a trans spouse support group. Depending on where you live, they most likely won't be in your town, but with zoom it is possible to join another one in another place in the country/world.
- A therapist can be a great support person if you find the right person. However, ensure that this therapist is actually supportive of your relationship and that you don't need to educate them. So, do your homework when interviewing them! You should not be paying to educate them.
- PFLAG is another place that can offer support and where you can find people to talk with who are going to be kind and understanding of your experience.
- AI programs (at the time of writing this ChatGPT and BARD are two examples) are one way of "talking" or "chatting" when there is no one that is an option. You do have to say exactly what you need.

You will also want to consider some practical needs and logistics.

- Do you want to be able to call a friend while the surgery is happening or the day before?
- Do you want a meal train?
- If you have children, how will they manage

school logistics on the day of surgery and the days following?
- What do you want to bring to the surgery center? I encourage you to bring a bag of goodies for yourself. That might include magazines or books you like, a blanket you enjoy, or anything that is going to make you feel more at peace.
- Do you plan on taking time off from work with FMLA to care for your spouse and household after surgery? Processing the paperwork may take a few weeks. HR should not disclose to anyone why you are taking the time off - know your rights! Yet, is your HR trustworthy? In today's environment, it's a valid concern. If the answer is no, work with your doctor to be careful about what is said on FMLA leave request forms.
- Consider your spouse's post-surgery comfort. Think about pillows, sleeping arrangements, accessibility of essentials like plates, cups, and bowls. Maybe move things to lower counters.
- For a while, it is going to be important that they pretend to have T-Rex arms! No lifting them up and stretching those scars! You will both be happier with the result.

Chapter 12

My next step in the plan was to tap into Family Medical Leave and take time off from work. Three weeks would allow me to be around to drive and take care of the children. It would also provide me some time for self-care and adjusting to the changes happening. This is not a valid reason for requesting Family Medical Leave, but I could request leave to take care of Jay, the children and the home, and this time away from work would help me too. When I went back to work after Thanksgiving, there would only be two weeks and then winter break would follow. This was ideal timing. It took some convincing the doctor that I would need longer than the typical time for the caregiver with this type of surgery. Initially, I think they only wanted to give me one or two weeks, but I pushed and got what we needed for the family. This was a huge transition for all of us, and with the support of Jay, my mom, and the therapist, I advocated for myself without guilt. My mental health was worth it.

For the actual day of surgery, my therapist and I made a self-care bag for me. She helped me take the time to contemplate what items would soothe and nourish me during the wait. I filled the bag with some magazines I might enjoy reading, watercolor paints, a template and instructions for my watercolor design, some healthy food, and a sweet treat too. We looked at a map of where the hospital was located and found a coffee shop nearby. We made a plan that I would be with Jay until they rolled him back to surgery. Then I would stay for a little while at the start of his surgery. After that, I would go to the coffee shop, which was less than 10 minutes away. I would buy myself a warm drink and spend a little time relaxing by reading a book or magazine from my bag. After that, I would return to the surgery center's waiting room, where I would work on a watercolor until the doctor called to inform me of how the surgery went.

Talking with my therapist, and others, we knew we also needed a plan for after the surgery. How would Jay sleep? Where would he sleep?

Jay and I both did research about what we could do to make recovery from surgery easier. We found many suggestions about how to sleep more comfortably. One suggestion was a wedge pillow, because after surgery he wouldn't be able to sleep on his back for at least the first few weeks. Another suggestion was to rent or buy a recliner. Other suggestions were to make or find a tiny pillow to connect to the seat belt so it wouldn't place pressure on his chest, especially right after surgery for the ride home. But also, for when he could eventually lift his arms again and start driving, about three or more weeks post-op.

Not really knowing what Jay was going to find the most comfortable, we decided to go with all the suggestions!

Jay found a fabulous wedge pillow that Joan uses to this day. Liz and I went to the fabric store one day and found some cute fabric to sew a pillow. We found a light blue covered in small rainbows and white clouds. It seemed like the type of design one might find in a pediatric clinic, uplifting and bright. Plus, it had rainbows. Liz and I watched some videos on how to sew the little chest seat belt protector pillow and made one with our sewing machine.

The only thing we had left to figure out was a recliner. So, one weekend, everyone piled into the minivan. Cole, Liz, Joan, Jay, and I took the drive to a La-Z-Boy store. We had never had a recliner before in my house growing up and I wasn't sure what we were looking for. In the car I suggested, why don't we brainstorm out loud what our perfect recliner would be like? Cole suggested we buy something electric, so we could tilt it back and sit it up with no need to pull anything with our hand. This made sense, because how else would Jay be able to control the recliner? Anything else I asked? Driving down the freeway, Liz thought it would be neat if the recliner had heat. Joan added, how about a chair that gives massages? Jay wanted the recliner to look nice in the living room, so maybe brown leather. In my ideal world, we would have all this and stay within our budget. We would see about that.

Parking the car, I reminded everyone that we were just looking and would probably not end up with a recliner that day. The most important thing was that Jay could get in and out of the recliner as independently as possible and that he would be comfortable in it for sleeping. We figured Jay would be recovering and resting during the day, but also sleeping at night in the recliner.

Walking into the store, a sales rep came right up to us and asked if he could help. I let them know we were looking for a recliner and told him what our ideal situation would be. The recliner would be in our budget, have heat, massage, be electric, comfortable, and fit right in our room.

The sales rep mentioned a floor model that he had available that might fit all our specifications. We walked to the back room and there was a blue fabric recliner that looked good. There were some recliners that would even help a person sit up. Then we saw the brown leather recliner in our budget, comfortable that had everything we were looking for.

We walked out of the store that day with a date set up to have our new recliner delivered!

By the middle of the month, I had a plan for the day of surgery. Jay's mom would fly up for the day right before surgery to help with transporting the children to school. My mom would arrive the next day, after Jay's mom left, and support us all for the next few weeks. We had a plan for where Jay might sleep. In terms of the logistics, we were ready. But there was something I needed to do before the surgery.

I needed to say goodbye to his boobs. I wasn't sure how to do this since he had been covering them up with a sports bra once he questioned his gender.

Jay's boobs were so uncomfortable for him, but they were a part of him I loved very much. I still didn't know how to talk about what I needed with him. I was afraid to bring it up and hurt his feelings.

Our anniversary was in October, and like many other years, we planned a weekend get-away. A friend stayed with our children, and we drove out toward the mountains and stayed in a cabin. The cabin was in the green woods of the Pacific Northwest. The rain makes everything green and bright, and moss grows on the trees. Our cabin had

Chapter 12

old pine wood ceilings, large picture windows and no close-by neighbors. There was a hot tub and deck where we could hang out, but it was raining so much we spent little time outside in the hot tub.

I felt all this pressure to enjoy our anniversary weekend, but honestly, I was a mess. I needed to take my anti-anxiety medicine because I kept on having panic attacks. I didn't want to take a lot of medicine that would make me sleepy, but that meant I wasn't taking a proper dose. My anxiety was nowhere near being controlled. Jay kept encouraging me to take a proper dose, reminding me it was okay for me to take care of myself. The doctor would say I should take my full amount. I would feel better, and I would not become addicted if I was using the medicine properly. But I continued to not take enough, so the panic attacks escalated more and more. When I finally took the correct dose, I was okay for a few hours and would think I'm okay. But the next time the anxiety returned, I would repeat the cycle and I would resist taking the proper dosage.

So, I had moments where the panic attacks were controlled and I could enjoy the beautiful house, forests surrounding us and the tranquility of being away from our three children. But those moments were fleeting, mostly because of my own fears of taking care of myself. On the second day, I finally made sure I took a proper dose of my medicine and that I didn't let it wear off so I could enjoy our vacation. We hiked in the woods all by ourselves, even though it was raining. Surrounded by old growth Douglas firs and cedar trees, we came to a little pond. Watching the drops fall into a pool of water was magical. The ripples of each drop spread out. I can still remember, I wore a green raincoat, but didn't have my hood up. Jay wore a blue raincoat and kept his hood down, too. The leaves and pine needles mostly protected us above our heads. Jay and I took some moments to kiss outside in the rain under the beautiful canopy. In that peaceful place, I let Jay know that if he was okay with it, I would like to take some moments to say goodbye to his chest. I tried to be gentle about the discussion, not knowing how he would feel about my request. We agreed that later that night, after a nice dinner, we could try to do that. It was important to me that Jay be okay with the experience, and I knew it would be extremely intense for both of us. After Jay came out as questioning his gender, I no longer interacted intimately with them. From that time forward, he wore a sports bra when we were intimate. I was fine with this, but I missed that part of him dearly. And it meant that I had never had a moment to say goodbye. They were just suddenly gone, even though they were still physically present. This would be my last time with them forever.

Jay agreed he would be ok if I had a last time to be intimate and say goodbye. After a quiet dinner at the chalet, we moved into our bedroom to have some special time with each other. I remember lying on my back feeling his boobs press on either side of my cheeks, just taking in the softness and perfectness of this part of him. I let myself experience all the joy, pain, sadness, and grief that came from this farewell.

This was goodbye sex. Goodbye to that aspect of his

body that would never again be there. I honestly still feel like crying when I think about that moment and writing about this time wells up tears in my eyes. Jay let me have that tender moment of letting go and being totally present with what would no longer be there. It was a magical moment. Both the strength that it took from him to let me experience that part of him again, and the presence we both experienced. I felt torn. I knew that being intimate with him in that way was something he was uncomfortable with. It was with an incredibly gracious heart that he let me have that experience and that we could do that together. I understood his relationship with that part of his body in such a different way, which made it hard to ask for what I needed. But bravely I asked, and he generously gave me that experience and time and space to process all my extremely complex feelings.

After, Jay held me as waves of emotions rolled over me. In the silence, we could see the majestic cedar trees standing tall outside of the bedroom window. In that space of silence, I felt that I had said goodbye in the best way that I could. I felt a sense of peace, as though a part of my heart had healed during this intimate goodbye with his chest one last time. We eventually fell asleep cuddling in each other's arms, Jay the big spoon holding me close to his heart.

After saying goodbye, I was as ready as I ever would be for top surgery day. Jay wanted the surgery done, like months ago. I mostly wanted the time after the healing to be here but was also terrified of how I was going to feel about his newly reconstructed chest. Would I be able to feel the same way about his new chest that I felt about his boobs? I had never been attracted to guys, not really. So, how would that be for me? How much of a loss were the breasts really going to be? Only time would tell.

With the countdown to Jay's surgery ticking away, every day was packed with a mix of planning and a storm of emotions. In these moments of intense preparation, my mind would often wander back to a memory that seemed more relevant now than ever—our honeymoon in Hawaii.

Toward the end of our honeymoon, we snorkeled at a cove known for its coral. Jay and I got out all our gear. He had special prescription goggles, because without those he can't see anything. (Remember the stars he pretended to see just to make me happy?) We also had flippers, so we could drift while gently kicking or put power behind our scissor kicks as we wished. We parked our convertible rental car (even though we were two "women" the car rental agency gave us an upgrade for our honeymoon, much to our delight and surprise) Strolling from the parking lot, through the lush tropical plants and to the shore, we took in the ocean. Waves gently lapped at the white sand. We breathed in the salt air and took in the wide expanse of smooth water, some breakers at what must have been the edge of the shallows, and then the calmer water out to where snorkeling boats brought people for day trips.

"What do you think about swimming out there?" Jay asked. I was on a swim team as a kid, as well as a synchronized swim team. It looked like an easy swim for both of us. The day was calm, and there were quite a few boats

Chapter 12

with groups of snorkelers out past the breakers. "That doesn't look too far from here."

Holding hands, we glided over the shallows. Through our snorkels, we observed tropical fish and more sea urchins than anyone would care to count. Careful not to get scraped up by the coral or to put feet down on the urchins, we held hands and glided together as we meandered closer to the breakers.

Reaching them, it looked like we were halfway between the shore and the scuba diving and snorkeling boats. There were a few families on the shore and floating in the shallows, and some day trippers out in the deeper sea, but it was just the two of us at the edge of the coral. We paused and looked at the breakers. The swells looked manageable, and just like with a sailboat or rowboat, we faced perpendicular into the spilling waves. It looked like we needed to get through a small stretch where the crests were plunging to get back into smooth waters. Putting our faces back into the water, we kicked hard into the sea. The frothy surf splashed over the top of our snorkels slightly, but one quick, exhaling forceful exhale cleared it out.

Kicking harder with our heads in the water, we made a push to get through the breakers as quickly as possible. We put all our force into our whip kicks. On the other side would be smoother waters.

But suddenly, a gigantic wave rolled up quietly and collapsed over both of us. I exhaled with all my force, but my snorkel didn't clear. Water filled my mouth. I swallowed some and spit out the snorkel. I treaded water to get my bearings and readjusted my gear. Still trying to clear the water, another wave roared over us, twisting and disorienting us both. I drank in more water, briefly pulled down in the undertow. Coming up again for air, a third wave boomed over us, again pulling us underwater. The wave ripped off my fins and stole Jay's prescription goggles and snorkel.

Gasping for breath, panic set in. My nose stung from saltwater, my mouth and throat filled with the burning of swallowing some.

I yelled for help, but no one was near enough to see or hear us over the waves. I started thrashing around wildly, wasting a massive amount of energy, no longer perpendicular to the waves. Tossed around in the surf, the water was way over our head. Without his prescription lenses, Jay couldn't see anything. He didn't know which direction would lead to safety.

But Jay could clearly see I was panicking.

He started yelling at me. "Pull it together! You can't lose it now. Focus."

His words centered my mind. I thought, *Okay, we can do this*. I started talking and coaxing myself.

One step at a time. First, we need to get out of these waves. Then, once we can breathe better, we will figure out how to get to land. The beach, which earlier seemed so close, felt quite distant without my flippers.

Holding onto Jay's hand, I directed us towards calmer waters. I positioned us, again, perpendicular to the waves, but this time heading towards the shore.

Without the prescription lenses, Jay depended completely on me for guidance. Having a job to do, I

Chapter 12

calmed down. One step at a time. I needed to hold his hand to guide him. That meant I was swimming without fins and only with one hand through the crashing waves. I attempted to make my way, swimming with one arm and no fins, doing a combination of freestyle with my legs and breaststroke with my one free arm. Every few minutes, waves filled my remaining snorkel with water. Jay had no snorkel, and so did his best to breathe in air, while putting all his strength into his whip kick, trying to share his momentum with me. Stroke by stroke, we made it through the breakers toward the calmer waters.

Still, so far from the shore, we needed to keep going. We couldn't rest by treading water without banging into sharp rocks. So, as carefully as I could, I guided Jay around the sharp rocks towards shore. Soon I was exhausted, but Jay could now help pull me along. Shore suddenly seemed so much further away than it had in the beginning. But together we kept on swimming until we reached a place where the sand was urchin free and shallow enough that we could stand.

Standing with barely any energy left in us, we caught our breath. I looked back out at the breakers. From here, they didn't look that big. The water beyond still looked calm, but I had no desire to swim in the open at that moment.

We waded ashore, and I crashed down on the beach, panting. Lying on my back, I let the Earth take all my weight while I recovered. I shook all over, realizing what a precarious situation we had gotten ourselves into.

We were both covered in gashes and scrapes from

where we had crashed into sharp rocks. But we were together, safe and on solid land.

Exhausted and sprawled on the beach, our breathing came in ragged gasps. I felt the solid ground beneath us and realized the full weight of our ordeal. It was terrifying, yes, but also a stark reminder of our ability to pull through tough times together. It was a reassurance, in its own way, that despite the unknowns of surgery and recovery, we had a history of facing challenges head-on, as a team.

Thinking back to that experience, I remember us nursing our cuts and bruises, but I can see the parallels between that experience and our current life challenges. Those unpredictable waves were like the unforeseen hurdles we were facing now, demanding resilience and mutual reliance. This memory, now resurfacing with newfound significance, was a comforting assurance. It reaffirmed my belief that no matter how daunting the post-surgery period might be, our strength as a couple would see us through. That frantic struggle to safety was a testament to our support for each other, a strength we would undoubtedly draw upon in the upcoming days. It was a mix of relief and resolve that washed over me then, a reminder of our journey through those Hawaiian waters and how, together, we could navigate any challenge life threw our way. We were and are a team, and we were ready for this next wave in our journey together.

Chapter 12

Recreate a Memory

Think a story during of a time when you and your spouse worked as a team. It could be during a power outage where you figured out how to keep the food fresh and wash dishes by hand, or when you got lost and turned it into a fun adventure.

It should be a time when you had to cooperate, and the experience was positive for both of you. The story doesn't have to be a dramatic event, but it should be a time when you worked as a partnership. Close your eyes and reimagine yourself back in that situation but reimagine it considering who you now understand your spouse truly was at that time. Relive the experience like a movie in your mind, or kinesthetically if you have no visual memory.

Expect a wide range of emotions, like grief, joy, pride, relief, and more. That is okay.

Try to let the critical, judgmental part of you go dormant.

Here's an analogy: If you were headed to a fancy dinner, and you suddenly remembered you had to move your laundry to the dryer, you'd tell yourself, "Now isn't the time to think about that. I'll do it later." If you can do that, you can use the same skill with this exercise. Shift your focus away from thoughts to how you feel in your body. Stay centered on your actual emotions, not on your thoughts about them.

As you reimagine the scene, float and relax into your feelings. It is safe to feel the nostalgia, love, connection, joy, or humor. You might feel a lightness or tightness in your chest or notice your breathing. Remembering the past in a new way helps you create new neural pathways. You might feel grief that the way you imagined your spouse has changed. That can and might feel like a loss. All emotions and physical sensations are fine.

After finishing, take some time to reflect. You might draw, write, talk, take a video of yourself or dance them out.

Then reset. That could involve taking a bath, listening to music with words and focusing on the words, lifting

Chapter 12

weights, taking a walk, talking with a friend, watching funny videos of baby animals, or engaging in a hobby.

In summary: Reimagine, Reflect, Reset.

Chapter 13

November

On November 1st, Jay received a confirmation from his medical team that surgery was going ahead as planned. He was scheduled to arrive at the surgery center at 5:45 am on the day of the operation. That would mean leaving our house at 5:15 am to get to the other side of town.

Excited, I packed my surgery bag and made sure it was ready to go. I put in my watercolor paints, some brushes, paper, and an outline of a rooster I was working on (Ahh, the irony).

For Jay, we placed the pillow Liz and I sewed into the car's seat belt with Velcro. Jay found an oversized zip up plaid shirt for easy on and off post-surgery. The shirt was extra-large so it would fit loosely over his drains. We took out the zip up plaid shirt, and Liz, seeing the shirt, decided to put it on. Then she took it off and put on all of Jay's recovery shirts, one on top of the next.

Liz started with one oversize plaid button-up shirt, then added another button-up shirt and finished with the zip up plaid shirt. Blues, oranges, browns, and greens all mix mashed into one very colorful outfit. Liz showed off her new finds to everyone by parading around the upstairs closet.

While she played dress up, we made sure the house was prepped and ready for after the surgery. New sheets were on the bed and wedge pillows were put in place, along with a big puffy pillow to keep Jay propped up. Now, if we could just keep the dogs off the new recliner! They were sure the comfy chair was a gift for them. There could be no dogs jumping up on the recliner while Jay's nipple grafts were healing, and while his drains were preventing unnecessary swelling.

Finally, it was the big day! Four days into November, top surgery day was here. Jay stopped going to the gym two weeks prior to top surgery, terrified that he would get sick, and it would need to be rescheduled. Thankfully, he stayed healthy. Jay's mom came in from out of town the night before and spent the night. She would get the kids up and to school and be here when Jay returned from surgery.

Normally, waking up at 5:15 am is difficult for me. But neither of us had any trouble waking up that day. Excited, nervous, and not really believing the day was here, we drove to the outpatient surgery center. Jay drove the car for the last time (at least for a while), and I enjoyed the ride. Now that the day was finally here, I felt excited for Jay. I chatted with him about how he was feeling.

Chapter 13

Once we parked in the garage outside of the surgery center, I asked if we could take a video. On the video, I interviewed him about how he felt about the day and the upcoming surgery. His excitement beamed out of him.

I knew deep down that this was the day he had been dreaming about for years, well before he ever realized he was trans. I wanted to record the day as much as I could, so we both would have a record of this momentous event.

Jay checked in and we were both able to go back to the preparation area. He was really nervous, even though they had prescribed him some anti-anxiety medicine. The nerves were not about if surgery was right or not! We were both clear this was the right thing for Jay. He was understandably nervous about going under anesthesia, the recovery, and how the process would go. A nurse handed Jay a surgical gown with green, silver, and gray squares all over it. It had snaps at the shoulders and down the front. He put on his surgery gown, with the snaps to the front, and sat down on the medical table. Less than 10 minutes after we checked in, Jay was under a space-age warming blanket, waiting for the surgeon to arrive.

Minutes later, the doctor came in and introduced herself, again, to us. She confirmed the procedure that they would complete and that they would use drains. Then, the doctor had Jay open his shirt and got out a blue pen that looked like a sharpie but was for drawing on skin. She carefully examined Jay's chest, started putting dashes down the center of his chest. Then, she began drawing the lines for where the scars would be and created a drawing of what his new chest would look like. She carefully placed where the nipple graphs would be located, reconfirmed sizing, and everything else. With Jay's permission, I recorded the entire process of drawing and marking him up.

The doctor then talked with us about managing his pain over the next few days post-op and the importance of alternating an acetaminophen and using the narcotic pain pills only as necessary. She gave me a prescription and suggested I fill it before Jay was out of surgery so we could head straight to the car after the procedure.

With logistics out of the way, the doctor said she would take Jay back soon. She left to prepare for the surgery. I looked at Jay, sitting in his space-age blanket and in his scrubs. I snuggled next to him on the edge of the hospital bed, the best I could.

With the moment at hand, I felt fully present, so in love with Jay and overwhelmed by his bravery. To have waited for such a long time for this. I felt so full of emotion and pride for him. I can't imagine how scary it was for him, each step of the way, to be true to himself. Not knowing what the consequence would be. Would his wife, family, children, and community stand by him and not just accept, but celebrate him becoming himself?

After the doctor left, a nurse anesthesiologist came in and inserted Jay's IV. The nurse asked if Jay might want something to soothe his nerves, and Jay agreed wholeheartedly with that suggestion. They put a bolus in his IV, and Jay grew a little sleepy, or at least more relaxed. His amazing silver space-age blanket blew warm air all around him and Jay settled down for surgery. To me, only a few

Chapter 13

minutes passed when the team started wheeling Jay down the hall and into surgery. I kissed him one last time and told him how much I loved him and how brave he was. "I'll be there as soon as you wake up and I'm allowed to visit."

I walked by myself out of the hall and into the waiting room. I went up to the pharmacy and took my number. Filling the prescription, I then walked back down the stairs to the waiting room for the four to five-hour wait.

What to do with myself? I felt a jumble of emotions. Excited for him, hopeful that the surgery would go smoothly, a little worried about complications, anxious about the grafts not working quite right and if he would be happy with the results.

There was a monitor that showed Jay's status with a unique number. I could see that he was back in the surgery room being prepped, but that the procedure wasn't yet fully underway. I was too full of energy to sit down and watercolor or read a magazine as I had planned to with my prepped bag. I paced back and forth a little in the surgery center waiting room. I tried sitting down and reading an article in *Self* magazine about Taylor Swift titled "Loving Yourself More", but realized after I reread the same paragraph three times that I still couldn't remember what it said. Maybe reading wasn't the right thing for me at this moment?

On the monitor, I checked Jay's unique surgery number again, and saw that he was officially in surgery! Okay, it is going fine. I just have to wait now, I thought.

I got out my phone and looked up the coffee shop I had

chosen. Not less than a half a mile from the surgery center was a Starbucks. I knew the team had my cell phone and would call if there was any issue at all. Things were probably going just fine, now that he was under the knife and the procedure was underway.

I put my magazine back in my surgery day bag and walked up the stairs, across the road, and into the parking garage. Driving out of the hospital and barely down the street at all, I parked outside of the coffee shop. I brought my bag inside with me and walked up to the counter. I ordered a soy milk decaf latte. I didn't need any caffeine to wake me up, even though it was still early. I was plenty energized for the day.

For a moment, I thought I should go back to the surgery center. Then, I reassured myself, they will call if there is a problem. There is nothing I could do anyway, and I'm less than five minutes away. Just sit, enjoy some coffee, and listen to the music. This is way calmer than being in the basement surgery center with its uncomfortable waiting chairs. I sat with my coffee by a window. I felt the warmth of the milk through the container and took some slow breaths. I smelled the fresh aroma and took a small sip of the foam. I watched the cars whiz by on the road outside, watching people coming in for their morning Joe and rushing back out to work and their regular life.

Part of me wanted to talk to someone, anyone. Any random stranger would do, even the barista. My spouse is having top surgery. What would they say to that?

Then I thought that would be totally inappropriate. I

laughed at myself, imagining how that conversation would go.

My spouse is having top surgery. He realized he was trans after we were married for 18 years. Ya, I know. Total shock. Anyway. Today is the day. He is getting a new chest.

Ahh (What in the world? Is this lady crazy? You don't just say things like that to people.) Ohh. Ummmm. . .

I know. I'm really excited, and nervous and I feel like time is passing sooooo slowly. And he is in surgery right now. . . I hope it is over soon and that his nipples get put in the right place!

I laughed at myself. I wondered how a conversation like that would really go. Then I figured the baristas probably hear all sorts of things. With the hospital close by, people must come in here to wait for many surgeries.

But I wouldn't ever do something like that! I was just amusing myself by imagining how that conversation might go. The imaginary conversation passed two minutes of the five hours I would need to wait.

Seriously, though, I don't think I wanted to talk to anyone that morning. I didn't feel like calling up a friend. I honestly didn't know what I wanted to do. I tried reading again, but I couldn't concentrate at all. So, once I finished my cup, I decided to head back to the surgery center. There, I found the closest parking spot to the surgery center exit. I walked back across the road, into the center, down the stairs, and found a spot with a kid table and stool. There were no children anywhere in the empty center. I put down my bag and thought I might as well try painting. I can't concentrate on reading, but maybe painting would be nice.

A few months earlier, I joined a monthly subscription to a water coloring program. Each month, I received paper, the watercolor paints needed, a video and written instructions for a specific painting. What came in the mail the previous month was a rooster with fabulously bright red and blue feathers.

I brought out my instructions. I hadn't even made a line drawing of the rooster yet. Normally, I use the template that comes in the watercolor kit, hold it up to the window to trace onto the watercolor paper. I couldn't do that in the surgery center, though.

So, I did the next best thing. I turned the sketch upside down and tried to copy the image the best I could upside down. I know that may sound strange, but I've learned that I am a much better drawer when I do things upside down. I don't know why; it simply is the truth. When I try to draw the right side up or the correct way, my drawing looks like a 5-year-old created it. I try the same drawing upside down, and it comes out halfway decent. So very slowly, because drawing upside down isn't easy, I sketched out a rooster.

At some point, I noticed I was a little hungry and took out an orange. I tried to peel the orange in one long circular loop. *Hey, that took 30 extra seconds. I have to pass those 5 hours!* I also had a little chocolate treat and then went back to sketching.

Before I knew it, my name was called. I walked to the door and a nurse let me know Jay was out of surgery and waking up.

"Did he do okay?" I asked.

Chapter 13

"The doctor will debrief you on everything soon. But yes, he is doing great and just coming out of the anesthesia now. He is in the recovery room. As soon as he is more awake, you can see him."

Excited and relieved, I put everything away to be ready for going back. I never even got around to painting my rooster! Someday I'll finish it, or maybe it was only meant to be a sketch. A work in progress, just like this entire process. At the time, though, I was relieved I hadn't removed all my paints. That meant I didn't need to dump out any dirty water, clean up any brushes or do anything other than put my piece of paper back into my surgery bag.

Walking back, I went into the recovery bay. I opened the curtain and walked inside. There were lots of "rooms" close to each other, but curtains separated each little recovery section.

Jay sat propped up in his hospital bed, ice bags covering the front of his body. His heartbeat and blood pressure were being tracked on the computer screen. I whispered, "Wow, you just came out of surgery." A slow, bright smile crossed his face, lighting him up. "How do you feel?"

"I feel great. I can't believe it happened!" Closing his eyes, he rested a moment. Then he sleepily opened his eyes again. "I can't wait to see it," he said in a very mellow, sleepy voice. Lifting his head off the bed for a moment, he glanced down at his body. "I'm all wrapped up in ice and my drains." Below the ice were compression bandages with the drains coming out of them. He rested his head back on the hospital bed and closed his eyes. Quietly, he said, "I'm looking forward to the recliner."

"Yes. You can spend lots of time in the recliner!"

"So happy to be with my amazing wife."

"I love you so much," I told him.

Jay then drifted back into anesthesia semi-wakefulness. Then, a few minutes later, we had a similar conversation again. He opened his eyes again. "Wow. I can't believe it happened. Did it go okay?" Slowly, Jay drifted from a semi-sleepy state to a bit more awake.

My heart was so full of love and tenderness for him. I don't think I realized just how much relief the surgery would give him. And so quickly, before his scars healed up. It was like when the butterfly landed on me in the garden. I realized Jay was always Jay. Transforming, but still himself at the same time. When the butterfly landed on me, I just held still, taking in the moment. I knew it was a magical moment, and I just wanted to be there, absorbing every sight, smell, sound, and feeling.

Well, I didn't want to focus on the smells and sights of the hospital, per se. But I felt this overwhelming protective tenderness toward Jay. I wanted to be there with his experience of pure joy and gender euphoria that came over his face as he woke up again and again to realize the surgery had gone well. Then he would smile with contentment and drift back to sleep. Honestly, I don't know how many times we had the conversation. But I still remember that moment with such sweetness.

A few minutes later, the doctor came in and talked about after-care. She had a calm demeanor about her and

Chapter 13

shared how the surgery had been a success and the grafts had gone on just fine. The doctor was talking to both of us, technically, but Jay was drifting in and out of consciousness.

She briefed me on how to empty the drains, track the amount being collected in the drains, and administer the medicines Jay needed. He had two drains sticking out of each incision chart. Every so often, I would need to empty the drains and keep track of how much liquid they produced. Jay can be squeamish about blood and things like that. The idea of having drains connected to the inside of his body freaked him out, more than a little. But I am not squeamish about blood and these things myself. I just wanted to make sure I knew what to do to take care of him and under what circumstances I should call a doctor. In retrospect, I wish I had videotaped the conversation because that way Jay could have watched it when he was more alert, and that probably would have been helpful later when he had moments of concern.

The doctor also talked about what to do with the nipple grafts—nothing. We weren't to take off the bandages or even peek. I wasn't sure how well either of us was going to do with not peeking, but knowing leaving them alone was important, I figured we could hold off. After so much waiting to have the surgery, now we would have to wait at least 10 more days to see everything! That shouldn't be too hard, and yet sounded hard, all at the same time. I know I would have been insanely curious about how everything would look, but also wouldn't want to mess anything up.

The doctor also gave lots of instructions about the ACE

bandage that was holding everything together. The gist of the message was do not mess with the elastic bandage, unless you are really, really uncomfortable. Then, if you need to, you can re-wrap the bandage. It should feel tight, but not too uncomfortable. Honestly, I thought it was wild that Jay was wearing an elastic bandage after the surgery. I knew that prior to the surgery, every once in a while, I would hear about how you should never, ever use an elastic bandage to bind. Because it could cause permanent damage. And now here we were after the surgery, and he was using one to heal. Somehow, that seemed ironic and a little funny. Perhaps, since there was no tissue left to damage, it was now okay to use a bandage.

Finally, we received instructions about the pain medication and admonishments to not use more than necessary. (Which of course would be hard to do since they hardly prescribe much anyway!) There were suggestions about remembering to eat enough fiber in the diet to not cause a new painful problem while solving the pain problem.

The hospital discharged Jay quickly. I put my arm around him as we walked up the stairs, across the road, and into the parking garage. I opened the car door for him, feeling protective, but also relieved that the surgery was a success. I just wanted to get him home so he could sleep for real. Jay sat in the passenger's seat. He was back in his blue-gray plaid shirt with a zipper. The large men's shirt fit over the drains and the ACE bandage perfectly and would give easy access to emptying the fluid. I adjusted the pillow Liz and I sewed. I snapped a picture of Jay, a huge smile all over his face, joy radiating from his whole being.

Chapter 13

Any of my tiny lingering doubts about how he was going to feel after surgery were totally assuaged. I knew this was the right thing before the surgery, but seeing his relief and pure joy after the surgery was still a huge confirmation of just how right this choice had been. I was filled with gratitude to live in a time and place where Jay could get access to the medical care he needed, that the insurance I got through my work covered this necessary procedure and that everything had gone so smoothly.

I drove home to where Jay's mom was waiting for us. She had made her famous cheese spread to be ready to make broiled cheese toast for the children after school. Greeting us at the door, she helped Jay get comfortable on the recliner. Turns out, the recliner wasn't what he wanted, so we moved him upstairs to our bed. Propping the wedge pillow behind him, another pillow on top of that, and tucking blankets around him, Jay found comfort and then drifted back into post-anesthesia sleep. Happy to be at home, he rested.

As soon as Jay settled in, Tango (our older dog) claimed a spot near Jay's legs. It felt like for the first 24 hours, anytime a person other than me came close to Jay in the bed, Tango would growl quietly. It was like Tango was saying, "I'm keeping him safe now." Knowing that Tango was protecting and keeping Jay company, I made my way downstairs.

I walked into the kitchen downstairs and chatted with my mother-in-law about the surgery and how everything had gone smoothly. She was off to pick up the three grandchildren from school so I could stay with Jay. He drifted in and out of sleep over the next few hours. I emptied his drains, tended to his needs, connected with the kids, and went about the rest of my day.

Soon, though, Jay realized the bed wasn't as comfortable as he had hoped. I very carefully helped him down the stairs and set him up on the recliner. The recliner would be his home base both day and night for the next few weeks.

The following day, my mom flew in. She worked for many years as an Advanced Registered Nurse Practitioner, and it was helpful to have her around the house. She assured Jay the drains were looking fine, and the liquid was the right color. She made sure we kept giving him pain medications around the clock as needed and had us create a whole timetable to make sure he didn't forget a dose.

Our friends sent us lots of texts to check in on how everyone was doing. My favorite one was from a friend who sent a GIF of a T-Rex trying to do pushups, with the caption, "T-Rex hates doing pushups." She also sent us a book later called, "T-Rex Trying" and showed a dinosaur trying to do various maneuvers with its little, itty-bitty arms—arms as useful as Jay's arms would be for the next few weeks.

As Jay made it through his first few days, and felt a little better, he would instinctively use his "T-Rex" arms more than he should. He would reach out or up. Now, I swear this was not my idea, but Jay's, but what ended up stopping him was putting a loose belt around his body just above his elbows. That way, when he started to reach up or

Chapter 13

out for something, he would be reminded that he wasn't supposed to make that movement. The belt worked like a charm. After a little while of wearing that, Jay no longer needed to use the belt to remind himself not to reach up with his "T-Rex" arms and was safe from stretching his scars.

Jay was determined to not stretch the scars. He had waited so long for the surgery, so much longer than the time he knew he was trans, in reality. He had wanted to not have boobs from the time he started to have them. So, he would not mess this up by stretching for a glass in the upper cabinets, or by being too active too soon. He would let his body heal at a slower rate to achieve the better long-term result.

The days passed in a daydream-like fashion. Lots of checking drains, and on more than one occasion, Jay needed to have his ACE bandage re-wrapped because the gauze would shift and become uncomfortable. Every time he would need to adjust the wrap, he would become anxious. I tried to balance validating his feelings while also reassuring him that as far as my mom and I could tell, he was healing up nicely. Jay eventually moved to Tylenol and Advil to control the discomfort. My mom did a lot with the children to keep them busy. I also spent time with them. The two girls and I painted together. Joan mainly drew for hours at a time in her room. Liz and my mom made use of my subscription watercolor box and created many pretty drawings that still hang on our art wall. Cole and I chatted and watched videos together. Time passed by and Jay healed.

For me, once the anticipation of the surgery was over, I could focus on helping Jay feel better. I don't recall having any concerns at the time about how I would feel about his chest or anything like that. I wasn't really focused on that. I focused on taking care of the family, being there for Jay and the kids, and feeling grateful that my mom had come up to support us. She had planned to stay for 14 days, but since Thanksgiving was around the corner, she offered to remain through the holiday, and we all thought that was a fantastic idea.

For Jay, the drains were terribly bothersome. It was hard for him to get comfortable, and he felt squeamish about seeing the blood. He also had high anxiety about pulling out the drains or if the nipple grafts were healing correctly. After the surgery, it was like all my anxiety had transferred to Jay. We all felt a tremendous relief when the day finally came to have the drains removed.

The day was a medium reveal date. We went to the doctor together, and Jay had almost unwrapped everything. He got to see himself with his new flat chest. There were visible bruising and scars, but I still felt happy for Jay. I didn't think or process how I was feeling myself about his new chest. That would come months later. But I was proud of Jay and protective of him. There was an immense sense of relief that the drains were out. Finally, Jay could wear a compression vest with Velcro, and we all knew that was going to be a lot more comfortable.

After the drains were removed, my mom and the kids joined us for lunch at a cafe. This felt like a celebration and a big milestone, our first time going out to eat after surgery. We ordered mochas, sandwiches and sat at this round table by a window. It was so nice to be out of the house as a family and to have Jay feeling a little more like himself.

Honestly, most of the healing time passed in somewhat of a haze. We thought we would watch a lot of movies, but that didn't really happen. Between getting three children to and from school, keeping up with the house, life and everything, the time raced by. Before we knew it, family had come from out of town to celebrate for the holiday.

By the end of the month, we hosted a pre-Thanksgiving Day meal at our house. We ordered in the food, because there was no way we were up for cooking for that many people. This would be the first time we would see most family members since the surgery. We had no way of knowing at the time that this would be one of the last times we would see family because of the pandemic that would happen in just a few months. Jay was well enough by that time to hold his baby nephews. He was still being really careful, but he could hold the twins if he was sitting down and they were calm. Observing their interaction, I had the thought that the nieces and nephews would never know Jay as anyone other than who he was right now. That is wild! Jay's brother and sister and our children will all have this sense of before we knew and after we knew, but the nieces and nephews were young enough that they would never have that dual reality in their mind. Uncle Jay would always be just Uncle Jay. Sitting down with soup, salad and bread, the pre-Thanksgiving meal seemed like many of the meals we had experienced in previous years.

We didn't know how precious this meal was that day or that it would be one of the last times we would see each other for a very long time, but what we knew was the love of family surrounded us. While not everyone understood what was happening at various times during the year, love still prevailed.

Chapter 14

December and Beyond

For me, sometimes it still felt surreal, like so much had changed and yet nothing had changed at all. Sure, Jay's body differed from a year ago, but the biggest change was more from normal aging. Actually, with T it was like Jay was aging backwards!

On the inside, what changes had taken place? On the inside, Jay was surer of himself and more confident. He was finding his voice. I know this is what Jay tried to tell me over and over from the very first day, but it just took me a really long time to understand. Jay had always been Jay. The person I fell in love with was the same person I am forever married to. I might not have understood all the aspects of how Jay felt about himself, but the essence of who he was did not change.

I think that is the most confusing thing about my experience with the transition. There were many changes, but so much more did not change. Jay was still the person he was when I met him. My understanding of him has grown. But at the end of the day, he was the same person who stood in an orange waffle weave shirt on my porch door many years before. My understanding of myself has grown as well. We are still the same two people who fell in love with each other.

One of the biggest and most noticeable changes is that the way the world views us is very different now. We look like a straight couple to the people we meet. And yes, that is jarring for me. I don't perceive myself as a straight woman, but Jay's transition has opened my eyes to the fact that my sexuality is a bit more fluid than I realized. Still, it hasn't altered my general orientation.

This is something that Jay and I talk about. We both have a sense of being a queer couple, and not a straight couple. Being in a neighborhood that is a mixture of conservative and more liberal people, we now look similar to our neighbors. Still, there is clearly a difference. While Jay is now the "man" and I am now the "woman" we have changed little about our day-to-day interactions, nor do we conform to stereotypes about our roles in our relationships. Much like when we were in a lesbian relationship, we do things around the house based on our interests and skills and less based on our gender.

On certain occasions, like attending a Pride parade, I feel invisible now. Since we appear to be a straight cis couple, it appears like I am a spectator. While I feel invisible on some days, that is a worthwhile price to pay for Jay to be himself every day. Everyone in our close circle of friends knows our relationship.

Chapter 14

I think there is a lot of variation around how couples with a trans man and female partner feel about their relationship. How we feel is specific to us. I appreciate that Jay typically wants to be out about being a trans guy to those in our lives. I know that might change with time, but it is something I am grateful for because it lets me be seen more fully in how I view myself.

Reflecting on that year of transformation, several themes come up for me regarding Jay's transition. First, Jay's realization that he was trans challenged me to learn how to communicate in new ways. I recognized I needed to become more independent in processing my emotions throughout the journey. In the past, I would share all my thoughts as they were happening, but with the transition, I realized that sometimes sharing was harmful to the person I loved.

I also understood that my own emotions were quite variable with time and that Jay didn't need to know every single thought I had and how I was feeling every time I experienced confusion, doubt, or fears. As a result, I became more thoughtful about what I shared, particularly when it involved negative feelings. I learned to wait and consider whether what I was thinking was something Jay really needed to hear. Through this process, I gained a greater understanding of the importance of boundaries and self-care in relationships. I pushed myself to connect with other people, go to therapy, write, express myself through music, and other forms of expression. These experiences offered positive effects on our relationship in the long run.

Throughout my spouse's transition, I realized the importance of thoughtful communication. I learned more about what to share through trial and error. In the beginning, I openly shared all my fears and worries with Jay, but I quickly learned that this made him feel awful and made him feel like I didn't fully accept him. While my initial fears about his transition were honest, I regret to have caused him pain and now try to avoid bringing up those fears. Looking back, I know I did my best and made mistakes out of fear and misunderstanding. No one is going to do everything perfectly, and that is perfectly okay and human.

My initial fears about Jay turning into a gay man and if I would still be attracted to him were honest fears. But I can't change the past. Now, though, knowing that those concerns were so painful for him, I try to not bring them up anymore. They are things that time resolved. Reflecting, I know that the mistakes I made were done out of fear and misunderstanding. Part of letting go of the past has been forgiving myself for the harm I caused along the way, knowing that I did my best.

Soon, Christmas day and my birthday rolled around. We were settled into our new way of living. For Christmas, Jay handed me a small box. Unwrapping the gift on that December day, a time marked by Jay's surgery and significant shifts in our lives, I found a glass-blown hot-air balloon inside. It was an orange and red globe that showed people floating in a hot-air balloon. Along with that was a note saying that the whole family was going to be invited along on this trip. The beautiful glasswork and the thought behind it instantly brought a smile to my face. Jay's gift wasn't just an ornament; it was a promise of adventure—a family hot-air balloon ride planned for April 2020. I hung the ornament over our dining room table, where it still hangs. The prospect of floating above the earth with my family, sharing this unique experience, filled me with a mix of excitement and warmth. It was a perfect metaphor for our journey, rising above challenges and seeing the world from a new perspective.

By the time April 2020 had arrived, we were in lockdown. There was no way we were going on a hot-air balloon ride to anywhere. I was teaching from home. All three children were taking their classes online. I had moved my parents from out of the country (they are expats) back to the United States so they could be in a country that had significantly more ICU beds should the worst come to happen. We still didn't know how the Corona virus was being transmitted.

Jay's transition moved from being this big part of my emotional concern to a little over a year later, being not much of a concern at all. It was now simply a part of my life and not one that caused significant stress, anxiety, or constant thoughts. I was much more concerned about how we were going to get our groceries, how to get all three children online for their classes and trying to teach students myself.

So there was no hot-air balloon ride to celebrate my birthday that year. We rescheduled for August, thinking that after three weeks, our lives would go back to normal.

We rescheduled again because of a flair-up of the virus and the company canceled the ride again.

Finally, in July 2021, we woke up at 4:30 am to drive to our hot-air balloon ride. Joan was up before I was. She woke up at 4:20 am and was excited about the adventure. Cole was up and ready to go as well. Liz was in a cranky mood. According to her, "I woke up in a rage." She couldn't fall asleep the night before and so only had three hours of sleep. She didn't want me to turn on her light, tried to cover her head with a blanket and was clear that she would not get out of bed. We needed to leave in fifteen minutes to make it for our lift-off time.

Jay attempted to get her out of bed too, but that wasn't happening. Finally, I let Liz know we were leaving on time and that we really hoped she was in the car with us, but either way we were leaving at 4:45 am. That resulted in her slamming her door. She is not an early morning person. But she got up and dressed and met us in the car.

Jane, our in-house DJ, had us listening to a way too loud, too upbeat song about a Neon Pegasus flying through the sky. But the song helped me wake up.

We arrived at the field to see six hot air balloons on a field. We checked in and were asked to help inflate the balloons. There were four other volunteers who helped us ready the 100 feet balloons to ride. They would then follow us in a truck and hopefully find us in one of the local farmer's fields after the trip.

We held open the balloons, and they filled with air. Not long after, we all climbed into a basket to ride the balloon.

Chapter 14

We soared through the sky and drifted around. Up and down, we saw two Osprey nests and floated around.

Once we landed, the same four volunteers were there to help us fold up the hot-air balloon. One of the women stood near Cole and Jay. She looked at both of them, and then at me. She asked Cole and Jay, "Are you brothers?" Jay smiled and said no.

Cole pointed at me and said, "They are my parents." (Talking about Jay and me).

The volunteer looked quizzically at Jay and me, and then me and the two girls. "So THOSE are your children?" the woman asked. "And you adopted HIM?" she said, pointing to Cole.

I smiled and said, "No. They are all OUR children."

The testosterone made Jay look a little younger than he was in the first years of transition, especially when combined with the facemask—an upside to the COVID masks. But he has some gray hair, so the lady obviously wasn't looking that closely at us.

On the positive side, the woman saw clearly that Jay was a guy.

He might look like a guy young enough to be the older sibling of our then 14-year-old son, but the point is, Jay looks like a guy. This is just one of the many awkward and humorous (to me) encounters that we have had in our queer family.

Later that day, Jay asked me if I noticed the lesbian couple that were in the balloon next to us. Jay noted that one of them looked sort of like he used to look, a more androgynous lesbian. We chatted about that for a bit and then moved on.

There are moments like this when we see a queer couple in a rural part of the state, where I still feel this loss of community. I don't love being invisible. I wish that there was a sign or a way that we could signal you're not alone and "Hey, we are queer too."

In the past, we would have made eye contact with them and acknowledged each other. Jay was androgynous enough that we would have been obviously a lesbian couple with three children. The other couple would probably have nodded at us and most likely there would have been a sense of being seen, even if we never talked.

But it is also no one's business that Jay is trans unless he wants to be out. And being out as trans in a rural town with random strangers wasn't the point of the day. We were enjoying a hot-air balloon ride and a sunrise to celebrate my 41st birthday.

In moments like this, I still miss that sense of being seen and that connection. There is a shared experience there and an easy bonding, especially when you come across another queer couple. We don't stand out as queer anymore.

But on the day of the hot-air balloon, it didn't seem like a big loss. That easy connection sometimes feels like a loss, but most of the time it doesn't bother me anymore. One big reason it no longer bothers me is that I now have friendships with other spouses who also have trans partners and so I have a sense of community and feel less isolated in my experience.

Chapter 14

Yes, we looked like a straight couple with three children. Yes, we looked like my spouse was way too young to have a 14-year-old child. We look like different things to different people.

But way more important than how we look to other people is that we are happy. I love Jay. I love that he is comfortable in his own skin. A stranger on the street will no longer know we are lesbians, but that is a price I'm willing to pay for having our amazing relationship. I love Jay to the moon and beyond. Our children have all adapted smoothly to this transition. To them, they honestly say they don't have many memories of what things were like before. They now have adapted from calling Jay "Mama" to calling him by his first name. It has been a smooth transition for them, and from their point of view, they had two parents who loved them before and after.

Being visibly queer isn't as important to me as being in a loving relationship where everyone gets to be themselves authentically. Other people don't get to define us. We are still close to a few lesbian couples that we have known for over a decade before Jay's transition. But we've had to work hard to expand our community. I am creating a strong queer community with other people who are trans or have a trans partner. This has shifted my experience in so many ways. The new community and friendships we have created are strong and beautiful. I have many new friends and new experiences I never would have had before. I am beyond thankful that we live in a time and place where Jay gets to be himself and express himself more fully, and that I could find support and make friends through the process. I also discovered new things about myself.

While writing this book, I had a lot of time to think about everything that's happened. Jay's transition was a big deal for our family, but it wasn't just about him becoming his true self. It set off a chain reaction for me as well.

As Jay started living more authentically and dropping aspects that did not work for him, I reflected more on myself, too. This was a slow process, but three years after Jay came out as trans, our youngest daughter got diagnosed with autism. Honestly, it was a relief by the time she received her diagnosis. We finally had an explanation for things we didn't understand before. But her diagnosis caused me to ask questions about myself.

Just as I immersed myself in learning when Jay came out as trans, I read anything I could get my hands on to better understand our daughter's experience with autism. The journey began with *The Asperkids (Secret) Book of Social Rules* by Jennifer Cook O'Toole, the first book I read on the subject. Its author, an autistic adult, presented insights that were strikingly familiar to me. As I read, I wondered why no one had explained these social rules to me as a child—it felt like I could have written it myself. This book first sowed the seeds of self-questioning in my mind. But it was *The Spectrum Girl's Survival Guide: How to Grow Up Awesome and Autistic* by Siena Castellon that truly resonated with me.

Reading this book out loud to my daughters gave me clarity and understanding. I recognized my own experiences mirrored in its pages. This book became my favorite resource, invaluable to both my kids and me. It was also written by an autistic author and its clear, relatable style made it easy to understand. I often reflect on how much of a difference it would have made to have this book during my teen or pre-teen years.

Reading books about autism, especially those written by individuals who share some common identity markers as me, was an eye opener. I started to question if the strategies I used daily were actually my ways of coping with undiagnosed autism.

From the very beginning of our relationship, Jay, ever observant and supportive, played a crucial role in helping me navigate social nuances. He was particularly helpful in practical matters, everything from cueing me to people's names to letting me know when I was info dumping to someone who was not interested in the topic at hand. An early day in our relationship, I remember wearing a pair of brightly colored, ankle-length socks made of cotton and spandex, which I found extremely comfortable. Jay pointed out that they completely clashed with my outfit. At first, I felt a bit embarrassed and defensive, but I soon realized he wasn't criticizing me; he was trying to help. As this conversation repeated itself over and over, I eventually wondered if my socks matched my outfit at all. This led to my epiphany about socks. To simplify my life, I switched to wearing black socks.

But why stop there? Why not make all my socks the same? So, I bought multiple pairs of the same black socks. It was such a simple yet effective solution. Now, any black pair matched with another, making things like laundry much simpler. Fast forward after Jay transitioned, I considered if I actually want to wear only black socks. While it was useful for me to understand the social rules around socks matching outfits, is this a social rule I always want to follow? There is a big difference between being oblivious while breaking unspoken rules vs. making a conscious choice to express myself in a way that is authentic. As Jay started expressing himself more authentically, I slowly started going on my own journey of self-discovery. So now, over five years after Jay's transition, I'm on a slow road toward unlearning some of my masking strategies.

I've always been someone who thrives on routine, and when Jay began his transition, it honestly shook up the predictability I relied on. Surprisingly, this change became a push towards embracing a more authentic version of myself. Now, I'm much better at acknowledging when I need some space. I've worked out a schedule where I'm able to have an extra day off a week. This change has been crucial for my mental health.

Reflecting on friendships, I've seen how my autism affected my interaction with others. My daughter Joan's sleepover story hit close to home. It hurt my heart deeply to see her process this loss for over a year, a clear sign of her autism and her struggle to grasp social changes.

This entire experience made me think back to my own past friendships and how painful it was to feel left out, not really understanding why. In my teenage years, I faced similar situations. I lost two close friends, one in ninth grade and another during my senior year. I was intensely focused on each of these friends, a trait common among autistic women, but I didn't recognize it then. Each friendship ended after I unwittingly crossed some invisible neurotypical lines. My actions, quirky and unintentional, were enough to push them away. We would now say that both of them ghosted me. I reconnected with both on a more casual acquaintance level years later, but the dynamics were never the same.

When Jay came out, these childhood experiences resurfaced, and I found myself gripped with an irrational fear. Part of me was terrified that I was about to be dropped and ghosted by my spouse. Even though it made no logical sense—Jay implied nothing like that—the fear and trauma from my past made it hard to shake off those feelings. It took a long time, well after his transition, for me to fully understand and confront these fears. Understanding my autism and reflecting on these past friendships helped me come to terms with my emotions during that turbulent time.

During the pandemic, a year after Jay's transition, I felt a bit more lonely than usual. Many of my friendships were tied to my job, and with all the changes, those connections just weren't the same. I also kept on feeling like I missed the more informal connections I had previously with the larger lesbian community. That's when I stumbled upon a webinar about adult friendships. That led me to an eight-week course by Shasta Nelson that really opened my eyes about relationships.

The insights I gained from Shasta's class were life changing. I realized what I was missing was a community of people who could truly understand my unique situation. So, I took a leap and used the skills I learned to create an online book club for spouses of trans individuals. This small step blossomed into something incredible—a book club that's been meeting regularly, offering support, laughter, and a space where everyone just gets it.

One topic that sometimes comes up is how social norms have shifted as our spouses have transitioned. My family's experiences have also highlighted societal norms and expectations. Because we had been two women, Jay handled the kids' logistical tasks, setting up playdates, talking with teachers, etc. This was huge for me, because that meant I did not have to do a ton of socializing in ways that were really challenging for me.

But after Jay's transition, we noticed changes in how people, like school staff and professionals, interacted with us. We started wondering, is it still okay for Jay to schedule play dates? Or should I also be on the texts because often other parents have unspoken rules and understandable concerns about setting up a playdate with a dad? It's complex, and I'm finding that I need to be more involved in ways that I did not have to be previously.

Now I'm reaching the part of my life where I think more about if I want to hold social norms. Maybe we are going to insist that the school and our medical providers contact Jay first because that is how our family works? Maybe we will include me in the text if we are setting up a play date, so we don't unintentionally make other families uncomfortable? Or maybe I am going to purposely mask

Chapter 14

my natural style and go with the social norms because that is going to help me with a specific interaction.

I am to the place where more and more often I can make a choice because I know what more of the unwritten rules are. I might wear a brightly colored rainbow twirly dress to work, but probably not to dress up for events. This is an ever-developing balance. How do I stay true to things that bring me joy while making conscious decisions about when I will break or follow neurotypical rules for dressing, talking, and behaving?

This outcome has clarified that Jay's transition wasn't just his journey—it was ours as a family. It transformed the way I see the world, seeing it through the lens of my autism. It's been a path of learning, understanding, and growing, both for me and for us all. This story, our story, isn't just about change; it's about finding ourselves while we grow and realizing the most unexpected shifts lead to the most meaningful discoveries. We've all transformed, and as I reflect on the pages of this book, I see not just our challenges, but our triumphs, our resilience, and the strength we've found in being unapologetically ourselves.

Appendix

Shifts in Intimacy

Let's be direct about this. Things shift in the intimacy world when a spouse realizes they are trans. That shift can be both dramatic and slow over time. It may include powerful feelings for both parties.

I also want to be clear of what I mean by intimacy. For me, I am including any type of interaction that is loving and involves touch. If your partner is taking hormones, there will be many physical changes that might or might not affect you. That ranges from hugging (hormones change how muscles and your spouse's body feels), holding hands (skin will change texture), kissing (pheromones and facial hair and structure might all change), to cuddling and more physical ways of connecting.

With or without hormones, how you choose to be intimate and what is comfortable may have small to dramatic changes with time. How that looks is going to be extremely individual. It will depend on how much dysphoria your partner has at any given moment, what you both are or are not comfortable with, your personal histories, and so much more.

What I'm going to suggest here, is more like exercises that can help to support you with emotions, feelings, and thoughts that may come up as you explore new things and have new experiences, like touching your spouse's facial hair for the first time while being intimate.

I will not talk about anything specific to me and my spouse. That is deeply personal and is not something I will share here. You should never feel the need to share that either. People might ask you things about this, but you never need to answer. Also, it is ok if this is something that you are figuring out. Over time, it will probably change. It is generally quite taboo to even bring up this aspect of conversation for many reasons, and even more so when one spouse is trans.

Exploration Experience with your Spouse

If your spouse is willing, I encourage you to explore each other gently and slowly as their body changes. Give yourself the time to re-experience things, as if it is the first time. This actually can be really exciting and a beautiful experience for both of you.

With the right frame of mind, you get to experience new relationship energy in an established relationship where you both already know you love and are committed

Shifts in Intimacy

to each other! How many people get to experience that in their life? No matter if they are going the surgery/hormone route, there might be changes along the way about how you relate to each other intimately. For example, if they have top surgery (well after scars have healed), take the time to gently run your hands on their chest. Or similarly, if they have new hairs on their face or any other change that is emotional for you, allow yourself the space to experience this newness slowly and in a meditative space, if you can. Even though you have been intimate before, I encourage you to check in frequently with each other about if you are both feeling okay. For both of you, this can also bring up powerful emotions, so be ready to take a break at any time.

Let yourself again move from internal thoughts, feelings, and images to external sensation. Go slowly and let yourself have the emotions you need to have. This is such a powerful experience, but must be done in a way that is positive for both of you.

If possible, notice the joy your spouse feels as their body becomes more and more comfortable. At the same time, allow yourself the full range of emotions. That does not mean you need to monologue or share the full range of emotions! Allow yourself to experience them internally, and then again shift to the physical sensation and visual sensation. Move away from the thinking mind and into the being space. This is where healing and growth will happen for both of you.

Know that you are both being extremely vulnerable and be very sensitive to that, on both your parts. Again, only do this if you think it can be done in a way that is positive for both of you. Then, if possible, share words of affirmation, or any sort of aftercare necessary for both of you.

Things to consider—when <u>not</u> in bed!

When talking about being intimate, it is easy to trigger a fight, flight, freeze, or fawn response, especially when dysphoria and identity are involved.

Some things that might be helpful:

Read or take quizzes on intimacy.

- Write about your thoughts, feelings, and sensations.
- Let your spouse have their emotions and as much as possible, not taking them personally.
- When dysphoria comes up before, during, or after being intimate, give your spouse the after care they need and take care of yourself too by writing or expressing in a way that doesn't escalate feelings.
- Schedule time to be intimate on a weekly basis and have a back-up night. This can help you experience the changes slowly and consistently across time. It can also help with relieving anxiety either of you may have about asking to be intimate.

A book I recommend for learning how to avoid the Fight, Flight, Freeze response is *The Declarative Language Handbook* by Linda Murphy. It is in no way a book about intimacy. It is designed for parents to help children with communication challenges, but surprisingly, it is full of wisdom that can be applied to this situation. What follows is a tiny piece of advice based on what I learned in this book but applied to a very different situation: how to discuss intimacy without triggering the fight, flight, or freeze response.

Moving from imperative language to declarative language can be helpful. Imperative language is asking questions, making demands. Examples would be:

- Do you like it when I touch you ___?
- What do you want to call your __?
- Kiss me ___.

Declarative language is descriptive and invites a response without requiring one. Examples might be.

- I like it when you touch me __. I'm curious where you like to be touched now, if you feel comfortable sharing.
- I'm wondering if you have some ideas of what to call __ body part that would feel good to you.
- I noticed you seemed to go quiet when we __. (And then wait.)

Discussing intimacy is challenging for cis people, and even more so when dysphoria rears its head. Be patient. It will get better. You both deserve to have your needs met. It is worth the time it takes to figure things out. This is hard, and it is totally worth giving yourself the time it needs.

Organizing Friend and Reader Groups

Before I go into the specifics on "how in the world do you get a friend group with other trans spouses," (Magic obviously) I want to share why a friend group is so important.

Here's the deal: unless you are crazy lucky, a friend group will not drop in your lap. I don't care who you are, friend groups do not just drop in your life as an adult. My middle school daughter informed me that this happened to her, but school makes friendships possible in ways that work life does not. Most likely, you are going to have to do some work. You will need to find or create a friend group yourself.

Trust me, it is worth it!

First, though, I am going to talk about why it is more than worth the effort. I know I had times where I felt very alone and like I needed to talk with someone who had gone through this. Other times I wanted to share something that was amazing or sweet or exciting.

In my experience, it is easier to become friends with someone if we share some similar experiences, beliefs, or values. When someone becomes a parent, they naturally connect and create a community with other parents. When a person is into gaming, they will naturally form close bonds and friendships with other people who share that same passion. The gamer can really understand the awesomeness of how the music and visuals create a satisfying gaming experience. They enjoy talking about their gaming experiences at length in a way a non-gamer wouldn't.

The same is true with having a trans spouse. Other individuals in long-term relationships with trans spouses have a shared experience unlike the experience of anyone else. There are aspects of our relationships that are universal. In reality, most of our family life is totally normal. Like, doing homework, teaching the children to be helpful, kind members of the family, doing the dishes, and deciding what to cook for dinner. Most of our life, despite what some people think, is not about going to public bathrooms. Our lives are mostly downright ordinary. That being said, there are aspects of our lives that are unique by having a trans spouse. Another trans spouse is likely to have similar experiences that unite us.

There is something magical about connecting with another person over shared experiences. It is special. I feel honored to have been a part of creating these friendship groups that have also been so nurturing and healing for me. There are stories I would absolutely share with any of my friends in my trans spouse's group that I might not share with all of my other friends from outside of that group.

Here is how I started the friend group…

I wrote up a flier about the group. I posted to a variety of closed online groups. There are many groups through Facebook that one can join. It takes some searching and many of the groups are private and unlisted. Not all are unlisted. I posted something like the following to one group:

> *Please join me for four one-hour long book group sessions talking about friendships. As my spouse transitioned, one thing I have missed is the group of lesbian couples I previously connected with frequently. I have been very lucky to continue with those friendships, but I would like to develop more friendships with people who have shared this experience. My goal is that we start to develop and/or deepen friendships with more people who have this shared experience.*
>
> *Four Dates: 5 pm - 6 pm PST Please only RSVP if you can attend 3 out of the 4 dates.*
>
> *Total number of people: Ideally, 4-6 people*
>
> *Location: Zoom room. I will give you the book club link after I meet you on zoom for 3-5 minutes for an initial get to know you chat.*
>
> *Book: <u>Friendtimicy - How to Deepen Friendships for Life-</u>*

Organizing Friend and Reader Groups

line Health and Happiness by Shasta Nelson. The book is available at many local libraries as either an ebook or audiobook. It was published in 2016 and can be found used online as well as on Kindle and at any bookstore. Here is an overview of the book so you can see if you are interested in this: https://www.shastanelson.com/frientimacy

How much reading is involved? You will read 2-3 chapters per meeting. (About 1 chapter a week). Please note that the author assumes the person reading identifies as female, but I have found the information resonates no matter the gender of the reader.

Who: Spouses and partners of FTM and Transmasculine individuals who are committed to staying in the relationship. It does not matter if you knew they were FTM prior to meeting them, just found out, or if your spouse is non-binary. It also doesn't matter how you personally identify. The only requirement is that your spouse or long-term partner is FTM or Transmasculine.

About me: I've been together with my spouse for around 20 years, and he started medically transitioning around 2 years ago. We have three children, and we are generally really happy.

Food: If I could zoom you food and drinks, I would. But since that technology hasn't yet come to pass yet (maybe next year!), feel free to enjoy your food and some drink while we are on the call, or not as you wish.

How to RSVP: Please email me at: YOUREMAIL-HERE. <u>Use the subject Spouses Book Group</u> *so I will see your email. Please let me know a little about who you are if I do not already know you.*

Please do not share this flier publicly. Thank you.

I created an itinerary to read a book together and meet four times. While I hoped maybe people would want to continue meeting, I did not start by asking for the moon! Organically, after meeting every other week for four sessions, most of us continued to meet.

About three months after meeting every other week, another person in the group suggested we move to weekly meetings. So, now we meet weekly and have done so for some time. People are so committed that we have had them join from hospital rooms, on major holidays and while on vacation. My friends mean that much to me. I look forward to our meeting every week. It is rare that no one can meet on our regular day, though we all miss a week here or there because of life circumstances.

But before I began the group, I needed to meet each person first. As people responded to me, I set up times to meet them one on one with them on Zoom. I did this for numerous reasons. First, I wanted to make sure the person was who they said they were. The last thing I wanted to have happen was to have someone who was actually transphobic show up for the book group!

Second, I knew if I was joining a group, it would ease my anxiety if I had met at least one person in the group first. I figured I can't be the only person who feels nervous meeting new people. Also, if I met everyone before the first meeting, I wouldn't be meeting anyone for the first time in a group setting! The screening Zoom calls only lasted around five minutes. Not everyone who initially expressed interest actually showed up for a zoom screening call.

Everyone who showed up for a zoom screening call, however, showed up to the book group. So, the screening helped me know when to stop advertising.

I also ended up having people interested in the group who didn't really fit my criteria. There were some people who were interested but had a spouse that was mtf. There were other people who expressed interest but could only commit to once a month.

Eventually, I created a second group. My weekly group is a closed group with only the original people from that first meeting. The second group is a more flexible group where people can come when it is convenient for them. We have even done Airbnb experiences together with spouses and are more of an informal social club.

I adore everyone in both groups!

The agenda below I wrote for my first closed friendship group. If you only create one, a small weekly group will impact your life in more ways that you can imagine. It is worth the effort and time. I promise.

For each of the four meetings, I created an agenda that

followed the same structure. After a few meetings, though, we stopped using breakout rooms because everyone wanted to hear what everyone else was saying! I posted the agenda in the chat, one item at a time. I also shared the overall agenda for each meeting with everyone. While this was a formal way of starting the group, it ensured we all got to know each other. Everyone shared the air space, and it gave me a structure so I could relax and enjoy the first few meetings without as much social anxiety.

After week 3, we ended up moving into a less structured conversation. By now, most weeks we start by having everyone share a little about their week and then, if we have time in the hour, we talk about the chapters of the book we planned for the week. These days, we don't always get to the chapters, but that is totally okay! We have read tons of books, and we stay on a book until we have discussed everything we want to talk about and then move onto our next read. Though we tend to move forward in terms of chapters, no matter if we have discussed the book or not.

First Book Club Agenda One

15 min - 20 min.: Introductions - 3-4 minutes per person to share a little about yourself. Here are just some ideas of what you might include: your name and pronouns, one word your friends would use to describe you, where you live, your partner/spouse, how you found out they were trans (transmasc or ftm, etc.) (if you didn't already know), one reason you were excited to meet other people with a trans spouse/partner.

5-6 min.: Breakout room (Groups 2-3)
What ways have you experienced an intimacy gap (if you have) to know other people with a similar experience with having a trans partner? How has that been for you? Or have you experienced this in a different part of friendship?

10-20 min.: Open discussion

First Book Club Agenda One

Does anyone want to share about something you have in common? What else resonated, or didn't from the book? Or wherever the discussion leads.

Last question: Everyone shares
One thought, observation, action, or insight that you want to remember or that you really connected with, etc.?

Logistics:
Please be mindful of confidentiality in terms of who you are meeting. Many of our partners are stealth, etc. Thank you!

For the next group, read chapter 3 and 4 and then choose <u>one</u> chapter - 5, 6 or 7.

Do we want to do a screenshot of our group - <u>not</u> to be posted publicly, but just for ourselves? Can I share everyone's email with people in the group?

Second Book Club
Agenda Two

10-15 min.: Introductions - (2-3 min. each) Share your name (we want to make sure we know how to pronounce everyone's name correctly!), then share one way you noticed you either experienced frientimacy since our last book group or made a choice to lean into greater frientimacy with someone.

5-6 min.: Breakout room (Groups 2-3)
Shasta describes frientimacy as "any friendship where two people feel seen in a way that feels satisfying and safe to both of them." She says it isn't so much how two people like each other, but how much those two people practice the behaviors that make-up a friendship.

Some ideas to talk about: In what ways does this definition make sense to you or not make sense to you? How has your experience of being the partner of someone who has

Second Book Club Agenda Two

trans affected how you feel seen in a satisfying and safe way?

10-20 min.: Open discussion

Does anyone want to share about something you had in common? What else resonated, or didn't from the book? Or wherever the discussion leads.

5-6 min.: Different breakout room (Groups 2-3)

Which of those three requirements are easiest for you right now? Which of the three requirements of friendship are the most challenging for you? Take 2-3 minutes for each person to share.

Quick poll:

- How many said <u>positivity</u> is the one you would most like to increase?
- How many said <u>consistency</u> was the one you would most like to increase?
- How many said <u>vulnerability</u> was the only you would most like to increase?

10-20 min.: Open discussion

- Why do you think x was the most common answer for our group?

- Do you think x is the area that most people with a trans partner struggle with?
- Was your answer a surprise to you in any way?

Last question: Everyone shares

Go around the opposite way from introductions (bottom of the participant list to the top). What is one take-away for you tonight? One thought, observation, action, or insight you want to remember or act upon?

Logistics:
Chapters for next time are 8-10

Thank you so much for coming!

Helpful Literature Resources by Topic

General Relationships

The Relationship Handbook by George Pransky was really helpful for me early in the transition, despite being a general relationship guide rather than one specifically tailored for trans individuals or their partners. One aspect of the book I found particularly enlightening was its discussion on the connections between our emotions and thoughts, highlighting how our emotions and thoughts reinforce each other. The book discusses how when we're feeling anxious or upset that the thoughts we have during that time are impacted by those feelings and vice versa. This insight helped me understand that as my thoughts and feelings passed, I would have different feelings and it helped clarify when it made sense to communicate what I was feeling with Jay and when it made more sense for me to take a break and just let myself process these emotions, recognizing that I would be much clearheaded once my emotions passed. This book offered valuable strategies for navigating communication and emotional regulation within.

The Seven Principles for Making Marriage Work: A Practical Guide from the Country's Foremost Relationship Expert by John Gottman is an incredible book that I highly recommend. It's not a workbook, but a comprehensive guide. It stands out for being very research-based, practical, and offering so many suggestions on how to handle conflict, as well as detailing the foundations of successful relationships and highlighting some pitfalls to avoid, like what he terms the Four Horsemen of the Apocalypse: Criticism, Contempt, Defensiveness and Stonewalling. I cannot highly recommend this book enough.

Intimacy

Tongue Tied: Untangling Communication in Sex, Kink, and Relationships is a really great book for navigating intimacy. It offers so many suggestions on how to talk about intimacy, which proves invaluable, especially as a partner transitions. During such times, some things that were once in your repertoire might cause dysphoria. Types of intimacy that are okay one day might not be on another day and that will probably continue to change throughout the transition. Having a guide to figure out how to talk about things in ways that are sensitive becomes crucial. Although not specifically aimed at trans individuals, I found it extremely helpful for me to become more comfortable talking about things related to intimacy.

Autism

Unmasking Autism: Discovering the New Faces of Neurodiversity by Devon Price is a book that, when I read, really helped me understand my perspective and experience as an adult with autism. There were so many things I related to in the book. I highlighted sentences and paragraphs, just like Jay had highlighted the book *The Tomboys Survival Guide* by Ivan Coyote. I highlighted a ton of sections in this book that really resonated with me. It was great to see so many of my experiences reflected in other people's experiences. This book helped me express how I was feeling and understand myself better.

The Spectrum Girls' Survival Guide: How to Grow Up Awesome and Autistic is another book I recommend. While its target audience is younger, it not only helped me understand my child's experience with autism better, but I deeply connected with its contents as well. I resonated with a lot of what was in this book, and it brought back memories, reminding me a lot of my experiences growing up. This book stands out as a valuable resource, offering insights and understanding across generations.

Memoirs from Trans Individuals and Partners

Tomboy Survival Guide by Ivan Coyote was a book that really resonated with me, partly because Jay had underlined sections that he really connected with. On top of that, I adored reading this book, and it has become one of my favorite memoirs. The narratives within are authentically written. The book features a range of stories that balance humor and deep emotional subjects. The personal anecdotes made me feel as if I was listening to a friend tell a story, thanks to the conversational and intimate writing style. I particularly valued how Ivan shared their journey as a gender non-conforming individual.

Queerly Beloved: A Love Story Across Genders by Diane Anderson-Minchell and Jacob Anderson-Minchell is unique in its exploration of a couple transitioning from a lesbian relationship to navigating one partner's transition to FTM. What sets this book apart is its narrative structure, where the chapters alternate perspectives regarding who wrote them, providing a nuanced view of their journey from multiple perspectives. I have seen no other book out there like this, and it presents an incredible story to read. The way it delves into the complexities of their evolving relationship, with honesty and vulnerability, makes it a fantastic book to read.

About the Author

Nuranissa M. Jones is a teacher and instructional specialist in the Pacific Northwest, where she lives with her spouse, three children, two dogs, and a cat. Her passion for gardening, playing piano, and being outdoors reflects her deep connection to both nature and community. Diagnosed with a learning disability in 4th grade, Nuranissa's journey into writing was profoundly influenced by a pivotal 7th-grade writing teacher who encouraged her to write freely, and not let labels hold her back or prevent her from expressing herself. This teacher not only inspired her own career in education but also her commitment to empowering others to use their voices. Writing under a pseudonym, Nuranissa seeks to maintain her family's privacy amidst the charged rhetoric surrounding trans issues today, while championing the transformative power of sharing personal stories.

Made in United States
Troutdale, OR
06/08/2024